SO-APO-673

JUST *Before* TIP OFF

MOTIVATIONAL MESSAGES FROM NBA CHAPELS

BO MITCHELL

Just Before Tip Off

Copyright © 2000 by Cross Training Publishing

Library of Congress Cataloging-in-Publication Data

ISBN 1-929478-13-5
Bo Mitchell

Distributed in the United States and Canada by Cross Training Publishing

Cover Photo courtesy of Lisa Hall Photography
Cover Design courtesy of Starwest Productions
Author Photo courtesy of Photos on Location

No part of this book may be reproduced without written permission except for brief quotation in books and critical reviews. For information write Cross Training Publishing, P.O. Box 1541, Grand Island, Nebraska 68802.

For additional books and resources available
through Cross Training Publishing contact us at:

Cross Training Publishing
P.O. Box 1541
Grand Island, NE 68802
(308) 384-5762
www.crosstrainingpublishing.com

DEDICATION

This book is dedicated to my wife, Gari, and our two children, Ashley Larson, and Andy Mitchell and to their spouses, Andrew Larson and Dana Mitchell, and to our granddaughter, Mackensie Larson. To all of you, thanks for being the greatest blessings in my life.

To Gari, I can't possibly express how much I love you and how thankful I am to be your husband. You are the most caring, thoughtful, kind, wise, and loving person I have ever known!

Finally, I dedicate this book to all of the NBA players, both Nuggets and visiting team members, who have participated in our chapel services through the years. I'm thankful for the friendships. I appreciate what each of you has done to enrich my life. This book is written in your honor.

CONTENTS

Post Season

Off Season

FOREWORD BY BILL MCCARTNEY

Chances are you have never had the opportunity to attend a pre-game chapel service. Because of my involvement in athletics, first as a player, then as a coach, I have participated in hundreds. Most have been prior to football games, but whatever the sport, there is always a dynamic of anticipation and electricity in the air. Emotions are aroused, and the tension is vividly real. Because of these complexities, few people are qualified and able to minister in this setting. Few people can walk the delicate tightrope that puts the gospel on the front burner, and yet keeps the impending game in perspective. Bo Mitchell is one of these people.

I have been a visitor to several of Bo's chapels with the Nuggets, and I am always amazed at the connection he makes with his players. He is the best I have seen, and I have seen many. He has so obviously been called and gifted by God for this ministry.

Bo brings the following four key ingredients to the compelling climate of his pre-game chapels.

Relationships–The long hours of investing in friendships provides the credibility that makes a speaker acceptable and believable in this setting.

Relaxation–Wit, wisdom and passion free the players from the task at hand and enables them to engage in issues of the heart.

Righteousness–Spiritual integrity is the component that renders a man alive to God's anointing so necessary in this super charged atmosphere.

Revelation means "an uncovering, an unveiling," or "a disclosure." The speaker is used of God to make visible something or someone once hidden.

As you read this book, notice how Bo disarms you with his humor, unique skills, and profound clarity. Then, whether you are an athlete or not, yield to the truth shared in these chapters, as your heart is fed from above.

Bill McCartney

ACKNOWLEDGEMENTS

In order for this book to become reality, I needed the support and friendships of many people. My sincere thanks goes out to…

Kyle Dodd, a gifted author, and speaker. Through his encouragement I was challenged to write this book. Kyle, together we've created something for me to leave behind! I'll always be grateful to you for your humor and motivational skills!

Todd Eley, the former General Manager of the Denver Nuggets. He first invited me to join the basketball support staff as the team chaplain. Todd, I'll always appreciate the fact that you were the one who asked me to step into this position, and then supported me through the ups and downs that followed. I miss our "pre-game prayer" and talks. You're a great friend and I treasure the memories we've built over the years!

Andy Mitchell, my son and co-chaplain. With the creation and launch of Garth Brooks' Touch'em All Foundation in 1999, I needed a co-chaplain to carry on in my absence on the nights I was traveling and was forced to miss chapel. You were my only choice Andy, and the players love you. Thank you for who you are as God's man and what you do to love, challenge, and motivate our players. Having you as my co-chaplain these past two years has made me more proud than you could ever imagine. Thank you for the time, effort, and faithfulness!

Dan Issel, the Denver Nuggets head coach and General Manager. Thank you, Dan, for the incredible opportunity you've given me to serve as your team chaplain. It's an honor to represent Jesus Christ and the Denver Nuggets in this capacity, and I thank God for positioning you as the leader of this organization. Our time together means a lot to me. Thank you!

Gari Mitchell, Ashley Larson, and Hallie Frantz were my three partners in editing and finalizing the chapters for this book. Thank you for your hard work and support in turning my style of delivery into something that people can read and hopefully enjoy. You are all wonderful and I will always be grateful to you for your help!

INTRODUCTION

In 1991 Todd Eley, the assistant general manager of the Denver Nuggets, asked me to join the basketball support staff as the volunteer team chaplain. Todd had heard me speak publicly and thought my style would be a good fit for the team. He also knew I had played baseball and basketball for the University of Colorado, and therefore my background in athletics made him think I had a clear understanding of the mindset of a professional athlete just before a game. In addition, the fact that I had earned a master's degree from Denver Seminary gave Todd confidence in my abilities to serve as chaplain.

After careful consideration of the time commitment—over 40 nights every season—I agreed to accept this position, and felt honored to do so. This has become one of the most fulfilling and interesting positions I have ever had in my life!

Over the years, a number of the players have asked me if they could have copies of my notes and handouts from some of their favorite chapel services. Just as I was beginning to assemble a package for a few of them, my friend, Kyle Dodd, encouraged me to respond to the players' requests by writing this book.

Since I felt it was important to respect the players' and coaches' privacy, no specific names are identified in the stories or examples I share. I also want you to know that many of the chapel services are on subjects that players have asked me about regarding situations in their own lives. You will see that each chapter tends to be short, to the point, with a story, a few brief scriptures, and an ending that is a challenge. This is the format of the actual chapels I present before each game. I have tried to keep true to this format as much as possible, so you can get the flavor of what chapel services are really like.

I hope that you enjoy this collection of messages. Please know that this book was written with the sincere prayer that you would be encouraged, uplifted, and challenged to grow in your own faith in Jesus Christ. Come join me for a time to focus on Christ, Just Before Tip-off!

Preseason

1

The Draft

The Denver Nuggets have two preseason games at home prior to the start of the regular season. These games are very important even though they do not count towards their record for the season. They are important because every year there are about five or six players who are trying their best to make the ball club. They are tenuously "on the bubble" and are looking for any opportunity to impress the coaches before the last cuts are made and the rosters of each team are set at twelve players.

The preseason games have also become important to me because I know that on these two nights, I am going to have a lot of guys at chapel, from both teams, that I may never get a chance to share Christ's truth with again. Some will be cut from the squad and will be packed up and gone before I even have the chance to say good-bye. With that scenario in mind, each year I take the opportunity in the first preseason chapel to ask the players, "Do you know what it means to be a Christian and have you made the decision to receive Jesus Christ as your Lord and Savior?"

As an introduction, I share a little of my background at May Avenue Methodist Church in Oklahoma City where I grew up. For fifteen years, I attended that church and never really knew why. I am sure all of the right things were being said, but apparently, I either was not listening, or it was simply not yet my time to truly hear the gospel. My family moved to Denver my junior year of high school, and I met Don Reeverts. Don had started a number of Young Life Clubs in Denver area high schools, and in the fall of 1966, he wanted to start a club at my school, Thomas Jefferson High. Initially we'd chat briefly, but soon spent quite a bit of time together. He came to our team practices and games, and I enjoyed his easy style and friendly manner.

One night, I asked Don to explain to me what it meant to be a Christian. He showed me these verses in John 3: 1-3

"Now, there was a man of the Pharisees named Nicodemus, a member of the Jewish ruling council. He came to Jesus at night and said, 'Rabbi, we know you are a teacher who has come from God. For no one could perform the miraculous signs you are doing if God were not with him.'

In reply Jesus declared, 'I tell you the truth, no one can see the kingdom of God unless he is born again.'

'How can a man be born when he is old?' Nicodemus asked. 'Surely he cannot enter a second time into his mother's womb to be born!'

Jesus answered, 'I tell you the truth, no one can enter the kingdom of God unless he is born of water and the Spirit. Flesh gives birth to flesh, but the spirit gives birth to spirit. You should not be surprised at my saying, 'You must be born again.'"

This time I understood what it meant to ask Christ into my life to be my Savior and Lord, to become a Christian. Maybe I had reached what is called, "an age of accountability" and was actually old enough to make the most important decision I would ever make. Or, maybe it was the fact that Don had not forced Christianity on me. Instead, he had become a trusted friend before we ever even discussed such serious issues. I am sure it was a combination of things, but after hearing Don explain that at some point every person must make the choice to either accept Christ or reject Him, I was ready to move forward. I recall saying something like, "Why wouldn't everyone want in on that deal?" Don's response was, "I don't know, it's kind of simple, isn't it?" I then asked Don, "What do I do now?" He said for me to follow him in a simple prayer. The prayer that followed included my confession of sins, request for forgiveness, and the request that Jesus come into my heart and make me a Christian by my profession of faith in Him. Just like that, it was done and I was born again, just like Christ instructed!

After sharing my story with the players each year, I explain to them how this simple message of love and faith from the Bible has been complicated by men for centuries. The methods used to present the "gospel message" often times hurt the listeners ability to comprehend this simple truth and causes confusion for people. I then ask them if they have already made the choice to become Christians. If they have not, and they are interested, I ask them to see me privately in case I have confused or challenged them in anyway, and then I lead them in the same prayer that Don led me in years ago.

Receiving Christ is the beginning. It is not the fullness of what it means to be a Christian, but it is the critical start. I liken it to when I put on my wedding ring to symbolize my commitment to my wife, Gari, 30 years ago which said, "I am committed to you, no matter what." In the same way, when we accept Christ, we say, "Yes, I believe, and I want this relationship with you, Christ, and all that I know of myself, I commit to all that I know of you!" At that moment, Christ's love and power take hold of our lives and "all things become new." (1 Corinthians 5:17)

Nuggets' players are usually guys who have looked forward to the NBA Draft their entire lives. When the day finally comes, some are drafted in the first round, others later, and some are not drafted at all, but sign on as "free agents." I point out to the players that in God's system, every person is a No. 1 draft choice. The Bible teaches in John 15:16 that *"You did not choose me, but I chose you."* He died for each of us while we were still sinners and then draws us to himself in a variety of ways. It is humbling to think that Christ comes to us as we are and has drafted us to be on His team!

This first preseason chapel, in many cases, is the single most important time in a player's life because many players have never previously thought about the decision to receive Christ until I ask them to consider the choice.

Have you made this eternal choice yet? Some people neglect to get around to it, while others reject God's love for them and go about their business. Are you in that state of limbo today? I encourage you to call a Christian family member or friend and seek their help in making this life changing decision! You will never regret it!

2

After You Are on the Team

There was great anticipation in Denver one season regarding a college superstar the Nuggets had signed as their No. 1 draft choice. It was generally accepted that this player would simply continue what he had started as a college player and would become a star in the NBA. His preseason performance progressed nicely, but during the first regular season game of his NBA career, something happened that negatively affected him with the Nuggets.

After struggling on defense for a portion of the game, our coach sent in a substitute for the new player. As the rookie approached the Nugget's bench after being replaced, our coach said to him, "Son, you'll have to play better defense than that if you expect to last in this league." It was an accurate and proper comment for the coach to make. The rookie's response, however, was not proper and revealed a poor attitude in the player that was harmful to the player himself and to his teammates. He said to the coach, "Listen, I'll play this game however I want to play it!" It turned out to be more than a comment made by the player simply in a moment of anger. It was truly how he viewed things. He had little or no respect for authority and was not interested in what the coach had to say. In fact, getting his way was more important to him than ever finding out what the Denver Nuggets style of play was like.

hat kind of an attitude, things usually don't work out for the better. Within a short time, he was traded to another team.

Professional basketball players know that once you are on the team, the real work begins! It is not enough just to make the team. A player must learn what the organization expects of him if he is to succeed. What are the offensive and defensive schemes? What style of play does the coach prefer? What are the rules I am expected to follow in order to fit in with the other players and staff members?

Finding out what is expected is required of every player entering the NBA if they expect to succeed in the league. In a similar way, we need to know what is expected of us after we make the decision to receive Christ. To answer the question, "What does the Bible say about how a Christian is supposed to live?" That is why each year I take the second preseason home game and spend chapel talking to the players about living the obedient Christian life. Notice I didn't say perfect; I said obedient.

Accepting Christ is the first decision a Christian makes. Next, a Christian must decide again and again to live a life of obedience. Obey what, you may ask? The answer is that to live in obedience is to follow the instruction, example, and admonition of the Lord rather than continue in the ways of the world. When we do this we *act* on what we know, not merely *talk* about it. This means that we accept and understand what Galatians 2:20 means when it says, *"I have been crucified with Christ, and I no longer live, but Christ lives in me. The life I live in the body, I live by faith in the Son of God, who loved me and gave himself for me."* No more can we even dare to *think* the words in the popular song, "My Way," much less live them out!

In the same way an NBA player must put forth an effort to follow the team's rules and instructions. As Christians, our *intent* each day must be to learn what Christ would have us to be, and then spend our days growing into that person. It is not a list of dos and don'ts, but rather an understanding of God's will for our lives.

First Corinthians 3:10 says, *"But each one should be careful how he builds. For no one can lay any foundation other than the one already laid, which is Jesus Christ. If any man builds on this foundation using gold, silver, costly stones, wood, hay, or straw, his work will be shown for what it is, because the Day will bring it to light. It will be revealed with fire, and the fire will test the quality of each man's work. If what he has built survives, he will receive his reward. If it is burned up, he will suffer loss; he himself will be saved, but only as one escaping through the flames."* What we do in terms of living obedient lives will be revealed with fire, and will either survive or burn up!

I am careful to explain to the players that I welcome them as friends, and I welcome them to chapel, whether they have received Christ or not. I also tell them I love them whether they are living obedient lives or not. They are not projects to me. They are people I care about deeply. But, because of my love for them and my responsibility as their chaplain, I am compelled to warn them of the earthly and heavenly consequences of choosing to live a life of disobedience.

The Bible speaks of the fact that the way of the transgressor is hard. Look at the lives of family members and friends who have persisted in their self centered, sinful ways. They suffer and bring suffering to those around them. I personally have messed up plenty and have brought pain on myself and family members for my immaturity and poor choices.

Ideally, we should begin to show signs of our Christian nature producing fruit that is pleasing to the Lord. Instead, many of us have needlessly complicated our lives through dis-obedience such as having an affair, getting involved in illegal activity, or simply mistreating others. The Bible warns of such conduct in 2 Peter 2:21-22 when it says, *"It would have been bet-ter for them not to have known the way of righteousness, than to have known it and then to turn their backs on the sacred command that was passed on to them. Of them the proverbs are true: 'A dog returns to its vomit,' and, 'A sow that is washed goes back to her wal-lowing in the mud.'"* The instruction of the Master Coach is clear and we will suffer consequences if we choose not to follow it!

For this very reason, make every effort to add to your faith, good-ness; and to goodness, knowledge; and to knowledge, self-control; and to self-control, perseverance; and to perseverance, godliness; and to godliness, brotherly kindness; and to brotherly kindness, love. For if you posses these qualities in increasing measure, they will keep you from being ineffective and unproductive." (2 Peter 1:5-8) There it is! There is the formula for living as God meant for us to live! If we want to be "effective" and "productive" in our lives, we must see that these qualities "increase" in our lives. What does He tell us to *do* to make this happen—He says to "make every effort!"

To do this, start by being convinced that it is all up to God. He came through for you and redeemed you when Jesus gave Himself on the cross for the salvation of all mankind. Then, by faith and in response to that act of love, live in obedience to the Lord. When you do, amazingly enough, you get the blessing here in this life and in the life to come!

Regular Season

3

Attitude

In 1994, the Denver Nuggets entered the first round of the NBA playoffs as the No. 8 seed in the Western Conference. Their opponent in the five game series was the Seattle SuperSonics who had the best record in the league and thereby were the No. 1 seed. At that point in history, no No. 8 seed had ever beaten a No. 1 seed, so the Nuggets went into the series as heavy underdogs.

Game one in Seattle saw the Nuggets fall behind 62-27 by half time, and Seattle's talent looked to be much, much better than Denver's. We went on to lose games one and two in Seattle, but then miraculously won games three and four in Denver on our home court. As I boarded the team plane to fly back to Seattle for the final, deciding game five, I noticed that spirits were high. The enthusiasm continued the following afternoon as we boarded the team bus to head for the game. I was one of the first to board the bus, and as the coaches, trainers, and players boarded, I noticed it was not going to be a normal pre-game bus ride. Everyone was talking and smiling, which is not the norm. Usually it is quiet as everyone anticipates the task at hand—especially the difficult task of winning game five on the road. I interpreted the relaxed atmosphere as a feeling of accomplishment and relief that we had pushed the heavily favored SuperSonics this far. It was almost as if we were surprised and were satisfied that we had won two games and had shown the world we were better than our No. 8 seeding.

The last player to enter the bus was our star forward. He is one of the most quality guys I have ever met in my life and is truly a strong Christian example. He also has one of the most intense game faces I have ever seen and an ability to focus like few men I have ever known. As he climbed the stairs into the bus, he caught my eye immediately, and I stayed fixed on him as he slowly began to touch the shoulders of his teammates and ask them the question, "Do you believe that we're going to make history tonight?" Each man would look him in the eyes, sense the seriousness of the question, and then respond by saying, "Yes, I do."

By the time he had talked to all eleven of his teammates, the bus was very quiet and *everything* had changed. Because of that one player, our attitude was no longer one of elation to be back in Seattle for game five, but one of determination to make history by winning the game!

Over and over that night, our team faced adversity. Our coach would rally his players, lift their attitudes above the roar of the Seattle home crowd, and get them refocused on the task at hand. The SuperSonics rallied near the end of regulation time, and tied the score. In overtime, however, the Nuggets won 98 to 94 and rewrote the NBA history books!

Often times, it only takes one individual to lift an entire group of people. One person's attitude can make all the difference! The Bible teaches that, *"Your attitude should be the same as that of Christ Jesus."* (Philippians 2:5) What? We can *think* like Jesus. Come on? You're putting us on! But, that's what it says. We can have His attitude—towards situations, people, problems, and opportunities!

I learned many years ago that thoughts lead to action, and actions become habits. The habits we live out in our daily lives help to shape our character, and our character ultimately determines our destiny. Our thought-life becomes all-important as to who we are and who we become as God's people. The protective shield of a positive attitude can lead us to fulfilling lives as God's people. We are to be salt and light to this world! (Matthew 5:13,14) We are to be encouragers and lifters to people who are hurting! How can we do that if our attitudes are not right? The answer is, we can't!

The Seattle SuperSonics probably never knew it, but the minute the Nuggets changed their attitudes on the bus that night, they had taken the first step towards victory!

"Your attitude should be the same as that of Christ Jesus: Who, being in very nature God, did not consider equality with God something to be grasped, but made himself nothing, taking the very nature of a servant, being made in human likeness. And being found in appearance as a man, he humbled himself and became obedient to death—even death on a cross!"

Philippians 2:5-8

Be humble, have the mind of Christ, and take your first step towards victory!

4

God is Able

One night during the dismal 1998-1999 season, I thought the guys needed a lift. They were putting so much extra pressure on themselves to win that it only made things worse. It was becoming apparent that during the course of each game every player thought it was up to him to carry the team alone. Guys would try to do that little extra to put us over the top, but the extra effort seemed only to emphasize individual play and not the team. The result of putting that pressure on an individual had the wrong results. We continued to lose.

At chapel, I began by talking about my own life. I wanted them to understand that there had been many times when my thinking had been wrong! Often I had thought that I was the real reason for successful things happening. I always tried to contribute my best, but it was truly God who was able, not me. He was the one who made possible any success I experienced. I shared stories like the time Jim Dixon, Bob Beltz, Everett Dye, and I started Cherry Hills Community Church in Denver. It seemed like a few of the Christian leaders in Denver were against what we were doing in 1981 and 1982. The truth was that the four of us, and our wives, believed that the Lord was leading us to start this church. Even if others did not understand that, the church was launched and God was and still is in charge. He used us to help build it, and today Cherry Hills has over 5,000 members and is a very strong, Christ centered church under Pastor Dixon's leadership.

A short time after helping to start the church, I set an appointment with a gentleman named Lon Lee who was the programming director at Channel 4 in Denver, an NBC affiliate. I told him I wanted to start a Sunday morning TV show called, "The Heart of a Champion." The format would be to interview Christian coaches and athletes in a relaxed setting, allowing them to share stories about their lives in athletics. Hopefully attracting a non-Christian audience, I would let the guest share openly about their faith in Christ! Well, within five minutes he said, "Ok, it's a great idea, when would you like to start the show?" I was shocked at his quick response. The launch of the TV show, however, and the success of Cherry Hills Community Church led me to start thinking that I was actually able to do some good in terms of helping others and getting projects off the drawing board!

A similar thing happened in 1986 when Richard Beach, the founder and president of Doulos ministries, started an inner city camp near Denver called "The Sky's the Limit." I was working at the time for Phil Anschutz, who is one of the most successful businessmen in the world. Phil, his sister Sue, and I joined Richard in launching the camp in just a few short months. The inner city pastors we worked with in Denver thought it would be a great tool to help train leaders from the city, and also give kids a great summer of fun at a Christian camp. It worked and is still working today with close to 3,000 kids in 3 cities per summer hearing the gospel of Jesus Christ and having a great time in the process!

Of course, I had more than my share of failures mixed in, but overall, the subtle message heard (from somewhere) was,

"Bo, you are able to get the job done for God, and God is smart to choose you to help!" What an arrogant thought! Looking back, I can't believe anything good was accomplished with me in the way. It was only God's grace and provision that made things happen because I was *way* off in my thinking and leadership style.

I explained to the players that I was completely distorted in my thinking—in fact, I was flat out wrong! Galatians 2:20 teaches us that "We have been crucified with Christ and no longer live" once we come into a relationship with Christ. It is not up to me, and it is not me actually doing anything on my own! If He chooses to use me, great, but my role is to do my best, while giving all the credit to Him. I believe I have never made a bigger mistake in my life than the one I made over and over by thinking *I* was in someway able to help God out by starting churches, TV shows, or summer camps. What an arrogant idiot! Who did I think I was?

A study in scripture on the word "able" proved to me even more convincingly that it was all about God and not me. He is the *only* one who is able!

God is able to:

SAVE YOU

> "Therefore he is **able** to save completely those who come to God through Him, because He always lives to intercede for them."   Hebrews 7:25

ESTABLISH YOU

> "Now to him who is **able** to establish you by my gospel and the proclamation of Jesus Christ, according to the revelation of the mystery hidden for long ages past..." Romans 16:25

HELP YOU

"Because He Himself suffered when He was tempted, he is **able** to help those who are tempted." Hebrews 2:18

KEEP YOU FROM FALLING

"To him who is **able** to keep you from falling and to present you before his glorious presence without fault and with great joy." Jude 24

MAKE GRACE (UNDESERVED FAVOR) ABOUND TOWARDS YOU

"God is **able** to make all grace abound to you, so that in all things at all times, having all that you need, you will abound in every good work." 2 Corinthians 9:6-8

SAVE YOU FROM THE "FIRE"

"If we are thrown into the blazing furnace, the God we serve is **able** to save us from it, and he will rescue us from your hand, O king. But even if he does not, we want you to know, O king, that we will not serve your gods or worship the image of gold you have set up." Daniel 3:17-18

HUMBLE YOU

"Immediately what had been said about Nebuchadnezzar was fulfilled. He was driven away from people and ate grass like cattle. His body was drenched with the dew of heaven until his hair grew like the feathers of an eagle and his nails like the claws of a bird. At the end of that time, I, Nebuchadnezzar, raised my eyes toward heaven, and my sanity was restored. Then I praised the Most High; I honored and glorified him who lives forever. Now, I Nebuchadnezzar, praise and exalt and glorify the King of heaven, because everything he does is right and all his ways are just. And those who walk in pride he is **able** to humble." Daniel 4:33-35;37

USE you

"For it is by grace you have been saved, through faith —and this not from yourselves, it is the gift of God— not by works, so that no one can boast. **For we are God's workmanship, created in Christ Jesus to do good works, which God prepared in advance for us to do."** Ephesians 2:8-10

I thought that I was just doing my best to contribute to God's team, but I missed it by a mile. It was not me; it was God through me. Our players, in a similar way, were trying too hard and not trusting God enough. This may sound like an incredibly difficult balancing act, but it is the proper perspective. We must know in our hearts and minds that God is able, not us. Then, we must work like it is up to us completely and let him use us for His glory and not our own!

Yes, give it your best and go all out! Yes, give everything you have to give. But no, do not think you are *able* to do anything, for the Bible says, *"Apart from me, you can do nothing!"* (John 15:5)

It is all about Him, not us. So live in a state of trust while putting forth an all-out effort and knowing it is Him using you, not you doing it on your own!

5

Bad Bounces

My baseball coach at the University of Colorado was a colorful guy named Frank Prentup. The "Chief" (as his players called him) was a very successful teacher and coach but had many peculiar notions about how to impart his wisdom to the young men who played for him. He also had unique one-liners that became branded on your brain almost immediately upon hearing them. One of my favorites from Chief came to me my sophomore year.

I was playing first base, and as I went to field a routine ground ball, the ball unexpectedly took what is known in baseball terms as a "bad hop." It hit me in the mouth hard enough to cut my lip, and the runner was safe at first. After the inning, I headed for the dugout still slightly bleeding, thinking that the Chief would meet me with a kind word like, "Are you okay, Mitch?" Instead he simply said, "What happened on that play?" I responded, "You saw it. The ball took a bad bounce and I had no chance to make the play!" He then put his hand on my shoulder and surprised me with his words of wisdom. With a slight smile on his face, he said, "Son, great players anticipate the bad hops and make the play with no excuses."

It took ten years before I understood, accepted, and believed what he taught me that day. When I first read the scripture, Proverbs 27:12, my mind went back to that baseball game and that bad hop. The verse says, *"A sensible man watches for problems ahead and prepares to meet them. The simpleton never looks, and suffers the consequences."*

It made me think, "Chief was right. It is possible to anticipate bad hops and then plan accordingly."

As I prepared for chapel one evening, it occurred to me that our players had been victims of a series of bad bounces in recent games. An official's call that went the wrong way—a pass that was slightly deflected—a shot that did not go in because the ball just would not roll quite the right way. But instead of joining others in the process of sympathizing with and patronizing the players, I decided to share old Chief's words of wisdom with them.

Chapel got rather lively when I shared the story of Coach Prentup and Proverbs 27:12. I said we needed to quit seeing ourselves as victims, but rather to accept the fact that things are not always going to go the way we planned. We all need to work our hardest to plan ahead and anticipate bumps in the road—then move on! But, I warned, we must not become *negative* in our thinking and *only* look for the bad bounce. My wife, Gari, points out to me that too much looking for the bad hop can result in what she calls "anticipatory despair." It is balance God wants us to seek.

I went on to share, for the most part, bad bounces in life can come from either people or circumstances. When people throw us a bad bounce, my advice is to be kind with the words you use to deal with them. This can be most difficult for our players during the course of a competitive game. But when Ephesians 4:26 says *"to be angry but do not sin,"* I feel the instruction is to choose our words constructively, rather than destructively.

I have not always done that, and I regret it. At times, especially in my 20s and 30s, I thought I was being honest or blunt, when in fact, I was rude, discourteous, and hurtful. If I could, I would ask everyone I have ever offended to forgive me. I would love to be able to take back things that I said and start over. Looking to the future, I hope to accept the responsibility for my words and think them through even more carefully before saying them!

In considering the fact that a few bad bounces will inevitably fall in their direction, my advice to the guys was simply—plan on it! Look for it! Anticipate it! Then, you "field" it better. Plus, do not get stuck in the "victim game." It is not always easy, but the Chief was right—the "great players" *prepare* for the bad hop, and when it comes, as it will, they are ready.

It is almost a guarantee from Christ when He says, *"In this world you will have trouble."* (James 2:1) You can look back on your childhood and wonder why didn't my parents do this or that? You can remember a moment from high school when you were mistreated and wonder why me? You can think if I had only been given that break, my financial net worth today would be much greater. Or you get a call saying your mom has passed away, or your child is sick, or on and on and on…

What will matter the most, no matter how awful the call, will be your decision as to how you ultimately react. Put God in the formula as you confront and deal with bad hops! He died to make you whole and healthier! Therefore, do not let anyone or anything convince you to continue to live paralyzed by the bad hops of your life!

6

Bring Your Best

My dad used to teach me that baseball was a team sport, but an individual game. He not only taught me the value of the team concept, but also the importance that each player should take the sole responsibility when he was alone in the batter's box or in the field. Basketball, however, "puts the most emphasis on team—you must work like a single unit in order to win," he would say. Passing, dribbling, rebounding, shooting, and playing defense are all dependent on your teammates. Games are lost when individuals lose sight of the team concept.

There was a particular point in the 1995 season when I felt our players needed to hear this lesson about the importance of working as a team. At the time, our players seemed to be playing in a selfish manner. They needed to be reminded they were a team, not just individual players. I also was excited to help them further understand the role God has laid out for them in life. We are all members of a bigger "team" called the Body of Christ!

As the guys gathered for chapel, I felt very encouraged that my message would be well received. I knew the power of the poem "The Cold Within" which I was going to share at the beginning. As you read it, picture a group of players reading it in terms of "Are we giving what we have to give each night to the team or are we withholding what we have for some reason?"

THE COLD WITHIN

Six men were trapped by circumstance in bleak and bitter cold. Each one possessed a stick of wood, or so the story's told.

The dying fire in need of logs, the first man held his back. Because of faces round the fire, he noticed one was black.

The second man saw not one of his own local church. And couldn't bring himself to give the first stick of birch.

The poor man sat in tattered clothes and gave his coat a hitch. Why should he give up his log to warm the idle rich?

The rich man sat and thought of all the wealth he had in store. And how to keep what he had earned from the lazy, shiftless poor.

The black man's face spoke revenge and the fire passed from his sight.

Because he saw in his stick of wood a chance to spite the white.

The last man of this forlorn group did naught except for gain. Only to those who gave to him was how he played the game.

Their logs held tight in death's still hands was proof of human sin. They didn't die from cold without, they died from The Cold Within

Author Unknown

Wow! The guys immediately responded by interacting with each other about what they had just read. It was thought provoking for all of them, and the message seemed to hit home.

As God's men the most important team we are on is the Body of Christ. First Corinthians 12:12-27: *"The body is a unit, though it is made up of many parts; and though all its parts are many, they form one body. So it is with Christ. For we were all baptized by one Spirit into one body—whether Jews or Greeks, slave or free—and were all given the one Spirit to drink.*

Now the body is not made up of one part but of many. If the foot should say, 'because I am not a hand, I don't not belong to the body,' it would not for that reason cease to be part of the body. And if the ear should say, 'Because I am not an eye, I do not belong to the body,' it would not for that reason cease to be part of the body. If the whole body were an ear, where would the sense of smell be? But in fact God has arranged the parts in the body, every one of them, just as he wanted them to be. If they were all one part, where would the body be? As it is, there are many parts, but one body.

The eye cannot say to the hand, 'I don't need you!' And the head cannot say to the feet, 'I don't need you!' On the contrary, those parts of the body that seem to be weaker are indispensable, and the parts that we think are less honorable we treat with special honor. And the parts that are unpresentable are treated with special modesty, while our presentable parts need no special treatment. But God has combined the members of the body and has given greater honor to the parts that lacked it, so that there should be no division in the body, but that its parts should have equal concern for each other. If one part suffers, every part suffers with it; if one part is honored, every part rejoices with it.

Now you are the body of Christ, and each one of you is part of it."

That last verse really hits home. "We **are** the body of Christ, and each of us is a part of it."

I went on to say that these verses made me feel great honor, responsibility, and challenge; Honor, because to be counted as a member of God's team was almost too great to comprehend; Responsibility, because of the desire to please God in all I do as a member of His team; And challenged, because of my desire to find out for certain what God expected of me as a member of the team.

I then asked the players to ask themselves the following questions: What spiritual gifts do I bring to God's team? What human talents did He give me that I should be using to build His Kingdom rather than using to serve myself, or worldliness? Am I holding back anything from God, like the men in the poem? Am I reluctant to give of what I have been given because I do not understand where I "got it" in the first place?

Well, by the time we left chapel that night, we had all agreed to give and keep on giving to help whatever team we were playing on—be it the Nuggets, our families, or other groups of people in the Body of Christ!

I challenge you to consider the last time you were given a great opportunity to give to the team but held back for some reason. Sin can keep us from aggressively giving, and eventually we can die in the process.

Therefore, choose abundant life over slow death and toss that stick of birch you have been given onto the fire to help the team! You will receive the ultimate joy and blessing! You will receive life!

7

Enthusiasm

I walked into McNichols Arena full of hope that this would be the night the Nuggets got on track and turned around a rather average season. As I went through my usual routine of greeting staff, coaches, and then players between 4:30 and 5:30 p.m., I began to notice that every person I encountered seemed to be discouraged, almost just "going through the motions," as they prepared to do their jobs that evening. It was obvious that it had been a long, tiring season, and people were disappointed with our team's results. Even though I felt sorry for all of my friends, I could not help but think about how sour the atmosphere was with everyone.

Oddly enough, I had prepared a message that night dealing with the incredible joy and enthusiasm we should feel as Christians. My text consisted of several verses that talked about the fact that "we really are God's children" (Romans 8:16) and how amazingly incredible that news should be to everyone!

When the 6:00 hour rolled around and the ball players began to file into chapel, I noticed almost no change in their spirits. I was becoming more and more convinced that everyone in the entire organization, especially the players, lacked passion, joy, or enthusiasm for anything—much less basketball! It was with these observations in my mind and my heart that I began to share how great of an honor it is to be called a child of God! I told them that the word enthusiasm actually comes from a word meaning "God in us" and that as Christians, we should be the most enthusiastic people in the world!

I went on to say that everyday we are *privileged* to live and grow closer to Him, and this privilege should be counted as a blessing and not taken for granted. I said with passion and in a rather loud voice that, "God loves us, is anxious to forgive us for our sins, and can make His grace abound toward us all day, everyday! Alright! Let's Go! Get Fired Up!" Their faces never changed expressions. Still no life, no enthusiasm. Finally, I said in an even louder voice, "God is looking for men who will stand up for Him and share His love with others!"

At this point I am not sure what happened to me but my frustration built to the point that I picked up the metal folding chair that was next to me, and in one huge motion, I threw it with full force against the wall and yelled, "Let's get fired up for the Lord!" Well, the chair fell to the floor broken beyond repair and the wall now had a good-sized hole in it. I was shocked by my actions and wondered to myself if I had totally lost it. I said, "Sorry guys I've put a hole in the wall." One of our most powerful players, a good friend who rarely says a word in chapel, responded with his great smile and said in his soft voice, "You also broke that chair into pieces." They all laughed, so did I, and the tension of the moment was broken. I then said, "I'm sorry guys. That won't happen again." Our team captain responded by saying, "Don't apologize, Bo. We got the message and the Lord inspired you to help us wake up—in more ways than one!"

Well, I offered to pay for the broken chair and the hole in the wall but our coach said, "No way. We won the game and played with enthusiasm—I'll take that trade any night!"

There are times in life when we do not feel enthusiastic about anything or anybody. At those times, look for a friend to "throw a chair into a wall," wake you up, and remind you to stay enthusiastic because you are a child of the Living God!

"Life is not an intellectual experience. It's an emotional experience. It's a feeling experience. We don't communicate with the world with words. Words are a secondary source of communication. We communicate with feelings, with attitudes. One of the greatest things you can ever do is to get excited today about your life and start to live enthusiastically day after day after day, and your whole world will improve. If you wait to get excited until some lucky outer event happens—guess what? If you wait, what does life do? It waits. And if you hold back until a more appropriate time to get excited, what does life do? It holds back. Listen, if you're going to hold back on your enthusiasm, develop lots of patience, because you're going to wait a long time for an exciting life.

When you become an excited person, you have an exciting life. When you get excited about your career, you get an exciting career. When you get excited about your relationships, you get exciting relationships."

John Maxwell

The choice is ours alone. We can choose to "just get by" and never really experience joy in life, or we can choose to get excited about life and the people in our lives. Even when we do not *feel* like it, choosing enthusiasm can change everything for the better! I encourage you to also make this choice, and watch the positive changes that will follow in your life!

8

Our Most Heroic Effort

A few years ago the Denver Nuggets took a road trip to Salt Lake City, Utah. The night before we were to face the Utah Jazz, four of the Nuggets players invited me to go out to dinner near our hotel. Before the meal was served, I asked the guys to share a story about their most heroic moment from a high school, college, or professional basketball game. Over the next half-hour I was astounded as I listened to them share some of their amazing stories.

A couple of them had scored 60 points or more in a game. Another shared of a last second shot to win a championship. I even pitched in a story about me playing for the University of Colorado and beating the University of Oklahoma in a college baseball game with a three-run homer in the bottom of the 9th. There was a lot of laughter, and we could not wipe the smiles off of our faces as we relived moments from our past that brought us pleasure.

When I returned to my hotel room and reflected on these heroic moments the guys had just shared, I thought about a phrase I had read in the May 8th devotional from Oswald Chambers' *My Utmost for His Highest*. At that moment I decided to scrap the chapel service message that I had prepared for the game against Utah and go in a whole new direction.

Chambers, in his devotional entitled, "The Patience of Faith," says, "faith is not a pathetic sentiment but robust, vigorous confidence built on the fact that God is holy love." He says, "Faith is the heroic effort of your life" and that we should "fling ourselves in reckless confidence on God."

At chapel the next day I asked the guys, "What does it take to be a successful NBA player in terms of the effort you bring to the court every night?" They all agreed that you could "leave nothing in the locker room, but had to give it your all every night, day in, day out, week after week, month after month, throughout the grueling season." As I shared with them Oswald Chambers' devotional, they understood that just as in the NBA, it took an all-out effort to make our faith the most heroic effort of our lives.

To be all that God wants us to be, we must attempt to "step it up a notch" and be sold out for Him and the things of His Kingdom. Chambers goes on to say that "shipwreck occurs where there is not that mental poise which comes from being established on the eternal truth that God is holy love."

There are parts of our lives that a lack of faith has not yet allowed us to give over to God. Problems can ultimately harm us, and a shipwreck will occur if we do not mentally dial in to the fact that our faith, which is to be a "rigorous confidence in God's holy love," is the key to finding the solution.

Acting on our faith and trusting God to do His part is how we are to live as His people. To do that, we must rise to a new level of commitment. The reward for living this way will not be the headlines in the morning paper declaring us as somebody special. It will not be an award presented to us at a big banquet before adoring friends and fans. The reward will be seen in the faces of those we love as they see us consistently treat them with love and kindness. The reward will come from inside of you as the pleasure of Christ grows in you to an unde-

niable level of maturity. It should be our common goal as
Christians to live by faith and to see it in action in our lives
daily.

To get there, we must exercise discipline and dedication in
the same way the Nuggets players do as athletes. Daily prayer
and scripture reading are the basic fundamental disciplines to
help us in our growth. Meaningful time spent with other
Christians also helps to encourage us. The challenge before us
is not to settle for being average in our lives as Christians any-
more than the players would be content to settle for being
average athletes.

God gave you His best when Jesus Christ died on the
cross. Your response to His act of love must be a commitment
to give Him your best, day after day, year after year, until that
final buzzer sounds, and you are called home to be with Him!

9

Aromas of the Arena

In the ninth grade I played basketball for Casady High School in Oklahoma City. I cannot remember much about my coaches, teammates, or how our team did, but I clearly remember the "smell" of our locker room. I know that sounds odd, but have you ever had a flood of positive or negative memories fill your mind simply because of a familiar smell?

As a professional baseball player in the St. Louis Cardinals farm system, I loved to run to my position in the outfield and take in all of the aromas of the ballpark. My favorite was the fresh cut grass. It almost carried me to a place far away from the battle at hand on the field that day. Every time I mow my lawn, the smell turns back the clock for me and I am a kid again playing baseball in Oklahoma where I grew up.

Most arenas in the NBA have their own unique packages of smells. In the old McNichols Arena, there was a popcorn machine in a small room near the wives lounge and staff offices. The smell of that popcorn would remind me of so many things almost every night as I entered the building. Then there was the locker room. Remember the smell of Ben-Gay? How about twelve pairs of game-worn basketball shoes? You get the idea. Some strange, but mostly wonderful smells, remind you of the fact you are in a locker room where gifted athletes are preparing to do their work.

I journeyed into this discussion one night at chapel with our players, and they knew exactly what I was talking about. They recalled many smells that they said they would never forget. Smells that impacted them positively when they came to mind. I then asked them if they had ever thought much about the scripture that says, *"As far as God is concerned there is a sweet, wholesome fragrance in our lives. It is the fragrance of Christ within us, an aroma to both the saved and the unsaved all around us."* (2 Corinthians 2:15,16) I then asked them to consider for a moment if our fragrance as Christians was sweet smelling and a welcome aroma to the people around us, or did it repel others with an offensive stench.

The Bible teaches that if we manifest the love of Jesus Christ and "tend his sheep" by loving others, our Christ like "smell" will be long lasting for everyone we encounter. If we grow and flourish as Christians, we should more and more be taking on His fragrance. The Bible makes it clear that people were drawn to Jesus. They wanted to be near Him. He had personal magnetism that can be ours when we follow His ways and take on His fragrance.

On the other side of the coin, do you have a memory about a person who has repelled you with his very presence? One season, the Nuggets had a player who seemed to me to be a lonely, self-centered, isolated, miserable man. I, along with everyone else in the organization, tried to reach out to him, but nothing seemed to work. I may have been the only one to see it this way, but by the end of the season, his personal "smell" had permeated our entire locker room and spoiled the climate. The season could not end soon enough for the fans, coaches, and especially the players. Our record was not too bad, but there was a "foul odor" about the whole season caused by this one player's attitude. It eventually drove one of the coaches out of the game because he got sick of "smelling" the same mess every day, all season!

What mess are you in today? What person or situation are you confronting daily that is so bad it almost smells sour? Or is it you? Are you the one bringing the bad aroma because of something in your mind or heart that is holding you back from having the "fragrance of Christ?"

Take a minute to consider the smell you leave behind when you exit a place. Do people want more or less of you? Christ says we can be like Him, and His fragrance is available to us all. Consider it, for yourself, and for all those you love and encounter!

Think of when you have reached out in an almost super-natural way to help a friend or loved one. Focus on a time when you had exactly the right word of kindness for someone in need. Maybe it was a unique gift that you knew would have meaning to a person in need of comfort. Maybe it was just the fact that you took the time to listen to someone who was hurting. All of these actions, words, gifts, commitments of time, left behind the sweet smelling fragrance of Christ, whether you knew it or not.

It is an honor to be called a child of God, and even more amazing that we can become like Him! I challenge you to leave behind the fragrance of Christ, for yourself, and for all those you love and encounter.

10

Commitment

A very old joke tells the story about the time a hen and a pig approached a church and read the advertised sermon topic, "What can we do to help the poor?" The hen suggests they feed them bacon and eggs. The pig thinks it sounds good, but he tells the hen there is one thing wrong with feeding bacon and eggs to the poor. "For you it requires only a contribution, but for me it requires total commitment!"

Total commitment today is becoming harder and harder to find. It seems like people are less likely to make a total commitment than ever before. Marriage is a great example. Wedding vows that state "until death do us part" have actually started meaning "until we run into some problems that are too hard to deal with." Fifty percent of all marriages end in divorce, and even the couples who stay together often times fall short of what God intended for a fulfilling marriage. My mother taught me that the commitment you make to your marriage will sustain your marriage during those rough times when the loving feelings that drew you together in the first place are missing!

In the NBA, talent, character, and team chemistry are the ingredients of championship teams. However, the teams that are almost unbeatable are the teams that share the commitment it takes to reach for the top prize and strive to be called champions. These teams usually have a coach who leads by continuously directing them to the commitment it takes to get the job done.

I have met some of those coaches, and just getting to know them briefly makes you want to play for them. They draw you in, lift you up, and motivate you towards a goal you maybe have not fully realized was there. They have an ability to impart to their players, and even staff members of their organizations, that it takes commitment to get over the top and be the best you can be!

One season, I was privileged to have every member of the Nuggets 12-man roster attending chapel regularly. This is very rare in the NBA. To have just four or five players attend is very good. But this team had a number of strong Christian leaders, and they were instrumental in encouraging the others to come. Knowing that many of the guys were either brand new to the faith, or had not yet even made a decision to become a Christian, I spent a number of chapel services talking about the commitment involved with being a Christian.

John Maxwell said it well when he said, "Until I am committed, there is a hesitancy, a chance to draw back. But, the moment I definitely commit myself, then God moves also, and a whole stream of events erupt. All manner of unforeseen incidents, meetings, persons and material assistance which I could never have dreamed would come my way, begin to flow toward me the moment I make a commitment." I use this quote to challenge any person who needs it to move out of "the gray zone of hesitancy."

Many times, players come to chapel as a good luck charm. Superstition has been a part of sports for years. Some guys think, "I will go to chapel just in case it can give me the edge I may need tonight." I am aware of this superstition, yet it does not bother me. I am there every game to serve the team. I am available for whoever comes to chapel for whatever reason. I am, however, comfortable pointing out to them that dabbling in Christianity is not wise. Lukewarm faith in Christ does not work for them or for God! Revelation 3:15-16 says, *"I know your deeds, that you are neither cold nor hot. I wish you were either one or the other! So, because you are lukewarm—neither hot nor cold—I am about to spit you out of my mouth."*

Having said that about lukewarm faith, I teach that an all-out commitment to Christ is necessary. It can mark the beginning of all kinds of wonderful things about to unfold. As Maxwell says, "The moment I definitely commit myself, then God moves also!" The Bible also teaches that a veil is lifted when we commit to Christ (2 Corinthians 3:14), and what had once made no sense, suddenly starts becoming clear. It is as if God waits for us to commit, then He turns on the tap for us! That is perfect love, isn't it? God is not pushy, but available and waiting for us to respond to His offer of love by making this kind of commitment.

However, I think this commitment is difficult for some of our players, and maybe even you, because there is some confusion as to what is involved in this significant commitment. Some people think, "Oh no, now I can't have a beer, dance, have fun, or be human—I'm now supposed to be perfect and I can't live up to that!" I have observed that those thoughts have kept many people from fully committing to Christ. There is a fear of the unknown and an unwillingness to receive His love because of that fear.

The fact is, God loves us and accepts us *just as we are.* (Romans 5:8) His love will never be any stronger for us than it is on the *first* day we commit to Him. It is at this point, however, that He begins to act in our lives and helps us to conduct ourselves in ways pleasing to Him. This is not a list of dos and don'ts or a life of misery. Rather, it is an abundant, successful, joyful life in harmony with the one who created us! The specific decisions about how we live our lives work themselves out over time as we learn from God what is and is not important to Him.

Other people are hesitant to fully commit to Christ because they want to test the water first and then jump in later. That is fine in terms of seeking the truth by asking questions of others. But as long as there is room for their retreat, there is a lack of total commitment.

Walter Henricksen in his book *Disciples Are Made-Not Born,* tells a story about commitment. "When Cortez landed at Vera Cruz in 1519 to begin his conquest of Mexico with a small force of 700 men, he purposely set fire to his fleet of 11 ships. His men on the shore watched their only means of retreat sinking to the bottom of the Gulf of Mexico. With no means of retreat, there was only one direction to move, forward into the Mexican interior to meet whatever might come their way. In paying the price for being Christ's disciple, you too must purposefully destroy all avenues of retreat. Resolve that whatever the price for being His follower, you will have to pay it."

I challenge our players to "destroy all avenues of retreat" and give an all out effort to win the NBA championship. But more importantly, I ask them to do the same in terms of their life in Christ.

Resolve that you will pay the price necessary to live in obedience to Christ. Go for it, and God will begin to move in your life. He will respond to you immediately when you fully commit to Him. Do not hesitate for one more moment. If you have tried to run your own life to this point, how do you like where you are today? Why not give God a chance—give Him your best shot! Make an all out commitment and you will never have to look back!

11

Shot Blockers

One of the greatest shot blockers in NBA history played for the Denver Nuggets for five years. He became a close Christian friend, and I will always love him. He had an incredible ability to block opponents' shots. He led the league more than once, and opponents knew that when he was in the game and you got near the basket, you were going to get your shot swatted away or, at a minimum you were going to have to alter your shot to get it off. It was fun to watch if you were a Nuggets' fan!

What is not so fun to watch is the destruction of life when well meaning, good people allow certain sin to persist in their lives to the point that blockage comes. My friend, Bob Beltz, and I developed a lesson plan called, "I'll be dammed." Obviously, our title is a play on words so as to help people remember the truths taught in the lesson. But the "dams" we are talking about are weaknesses or sins that can block the flow of "living water" in our lives that Jesus talks about in John 7 when it says, *"If anyone is thirsty, let him come to me and drink. Whoever believes in me, as the scripture has said, streams of living water will flow from within him."*

When I would have a chapel on this subject, the players would be challenged to identify if they had any "dams" that were holding them back.

Read through the list for yourself and see if any of these are "shot blockers" or "dams" for you.

Shot Blockers

LUST - My mind is triggered by stimuli and I seek self-gratification. Whether the action follows the thought does not matter to God.

IDOLATRY – I am guilty of idolatry when I permit anything to come between me and the Lord—family situations, income, position, amusements—to name a few.

LAZINESS – Taking it easy, frequently using tiredness, overwork, and other commitments as excuses for not investing myself wholeheartedly in whatever I am doing.

TOUCHINESS – Frequent resentment when someone disagrees with me—mate, child, employee, fellow Christian. How do I react when I hear what someone has said about me?

JUDGMENTALISM – Measure others by myself on matters such as dress, speech, cars, houses, vacations, use of time; quickly get upset when others behave differently than me.

GOSSIP – Have I let my tongue "slip" with comments that shouldn't be said or disguised these comments even to myself with thoughts of "It's best that they know this," or "Perhaps you should be praying for so and so," or "It's my job to check this out."

WORRY – Anxious about the future? Health? Bills? Family? Any mental stress which suggests that God cannot handle any problem or has overlooked something is godless worry.

PESSIMISM – Negative thoughts and feelings about life—Am I hard to please? I find it easy to complain about job, mate, neighborhood, and anything I am involved in.

DOUBT – From time to time I begin to wonder about things—Christianity, love, life. Is it all a big hoax?

SELFISHNESS – Want the best bargain in everything, the biggest piece, be the first in line, often impatient and ignore the interests of others.

DISTRACTION – Can't seem to focus on Christ. Hard to read the Bible and make sense out of it. Days fly by with nothing done. No definite plan for serving the Lord.

LYING – I seem to get carried away when telling something, blow things out of proportion and add a little to that which I tell.

DISSATISFIED – Restless at home. Perhaps a change in jobs, neighborhood, or church is what is needed. I wish I could get away from it all for a while.

EASILY DISCOURAGED – I retreat at the first sign of failure; give up easily; tend to quit when things turn out to be harder than I first supposed.

WASTEFULNESS – I squander hours on myself – TV, putter with hobbies, etc. when I could be working on my relationship with Christ, family, friends, or fellow man.

ABUSIVE – Weak temper control; speak my mind regardless how it might affect others; take advantage of position.

COVETOUS – I spend considerable time and energy dreaming of things and trying to get things that I see others enjoying.

DEPRESSION – Disappointments seem to overtake me and cause despair and sullen moods that cloud over everything. Problems seem insurmountable. I allow the difficulties, hurts, failures of the past to affect where I am today.

FEARS – Afraid of being embarrassed in business, to speak out for Christ, death, loneliness, sickness, etc.? Or maybe I do not know what it is I fear—I am just afraid.

PROCRASTINATION – I want to get involved in a deeper life with Christ, but today isn't the day to start it. Let's put this off until the time is better for me. Tomorrow will be better for this than today.

Hopefully, identifying areas that are causing you problems can be the first step to getting away from your "shot blockers," your "dams." Obviously, there are more than just the ones listed here. If you feel blocked, but cannot even identify the source of the problem, ask God in prayer to reveal the problem to you. Often times, identifying the problem is the first step towards the solution. In fact, Albert Einstein said something to the effect that 50 percent of the solution to a problem can be in clearly defining what the problem is.

If blockage continues and the joy is being sapped out of your life because you just cannot get past this particular problem, I would encourage you to set an appointment to see a pastor, friend, or a Christian counselor. Help is available, but consider carefully where you go for that help and rest in the truth that God will assist you every step of the way when we seek His wisdom. He wants your "shots" to go in and your "dams" to be broken.

12

The Game Plan for Life

When my son, Andy, was in high school, the varsity basketball team made it to the state playoffs. He was a freshman and was not playing in the game but sat on the bench with the other underclassmen. With only a few seconds left in regulation time, I saw something I had never seen before in a game. It led to a Littleton High School victory.

With only a few seconds on the clock, Littleton was inbounding the ball from the opponent's end of the court. To throw it in and travel the length of the floor, stop and shoot would be almost impossible. The player positioned to throw the ball in was named Jeff. Instead of throwing the ball in to a teammate, he stretched his arms out, over the inbounds line, while still holding onto the ball. He actually taunted the opposing player by putting the ball right in front of the other guy. The opponent's instinctive response was to knock the ball out of Jeff's hands.

Immediately, the referee blew the whistle and called a technical foul on the guy for "touching the ball while still in the possession of his opponent inbounding the ball." Wow! I could not believe my eyes as Jeff slowly walked the length of the court and made the two free throws to put the game into overtime and give Littleton the chance to win. The opponents were stunned. I was even more amazed when I learned that the Littleton coach had actually practiced the play for months, looking for the right opportunity to use it in a game! The coach knew the rules, and his knowledge of the rules helped his team come out victorious.

God has given us a "rule book" to help us find the right ways to win in our lives as Christians. The Bible is the "game plan for life," full of instruction as to how we are to live as God's people.

Once a year in chapel, I talk about the Bible and it's importance to the Nuggets players. I begin by asking them this question: If someone interrupted us right now with an urgent message that God Himself was sitting across the hall in one of the other locker rooms and was waiting to have a private meeting with you, how many of you would stand up, leave the rest of us behind, and head off to meet with Him? Of course, they all raise their hands, as would anyone.

The point I make with the players is that God does exactly that for us everyday of our lives by the availability of His Holy Scripture to read and study. The Bible is His way of revealing to us who He is and what His Kingdom is about. The Bible is our personal love letter from God, and if we view it that way, we will want to read and study it. Romans 10:17 says that, *"Faith comes from hearing the message, and the message is heard through the word of Christ."*

The Bible is also our protection from drifting into lives of sin. David says in Psalm 119:11, *"I have hidden your word in my heart, that I might not sin against you."* This means that we are to become so familiar with God's Word that it becomes a part of us, so that when situations arise where we are tempted to sin we remember God's word and we go the other way. Jesus Christ is the Living Word of God and we should never lose sight of the fact that *"your word is a lamp to my feet and a light for my path."* Psalm 119:105

Personally, I spend too much time reading the morning paper or my favorite magazines. I share the idea with the Nuggets players that some reading of that nature is fine. It must not, however, replace time which should be spent reading the Bible for enjoyment and studying it for personal wisdom and growth. There is no excuse for not knowing what the Bible says.

Many people spend too much time discussing or analyzing what other people say and teach about the Bible rather than digging in and reading it for themselves. I have asked hundreds of people, "Do you know what one percent of the Bible says? They answer with a "No, not really, because we do not know a good way as to how to go about reading the Bible." Many times I have explained that the Old Testament can be read as the necessary background to better understand the Gospels found in the New Testament.

But, if you get bogged down in the Old Testament, do not sweat it. Jump over to the New Testament and begin by reading the book of John. Then go back to the Old Testament and read one chapter in Proverbs for every 31 days of any given month. You can learn lessons on love, sacrifice, and obedience by studying the lives of Moses, Daniel, Noah, and other great Old Testament characters. In the New Testament, the accounts of Christ's life in the gospels and the writings of Paul will give you enough "solid food" to last your lifetime. God's word has been continually protected through the ages. It should be the source of life changing and life shaping information for everyone.

It is time to reduce the time you spend in front of your TV sets or reading your papers. It is time to turn off your computer and pick up your Bible. The answer to every question you have about life is found in the Bible. Christ will show you what is expected of you in your love for Him and will show you how to do a better job of loving each other.

The Game Plan is very clear, and each of us would live better lives if we would give it a chance. In a world full of opinions about every subject that you can imagine, is it not worth finding out for yourself if there is an *absolute* truth in the Word of God? I guarantee you, it is all there waiting to come alive for each one of us!

13

Getting off of our "Buts"

My friend, Bobb Biehl, is a tremendous communicator and a very gifted author who has written more than 20 books on a variety of subjects. He is also one of the finest Christian consultants in the world. He consults with leaders of business, industry, and ministry, and his client list is a who's who in terms of success stories. Gari and I became friends with Bobb during one of the most difficult periods of our lives. Through the crucible of fire, we have become lifelong friends. I have literally learned more from Bobb's pool of wisdom than I have from anyone else except my wife.

During one of our tough times, he advised me to create and maintain a list of personal positive accomplishments. His purpose in having me write such a list was to remind me, as often as I needed to, that I was experiencing a brief down time, yet my entire life has not been negative.

The positive accomplishment list, which I now refer to as my P.A.L., is a reminder of what Gari and I have accomplished in life. It is a useful tool to give a "big picture" glance at our lives, rather than being consumed by whatever negative situation may be confronting us at the time. Bobb teaches that everyone has bumps in the road, yet everyone also has a positive accomplishment list. If we will take the time to think about it, write it down, carry it with us, and look at it now and then, it can help give us clear continuing perspective and hope!

I am constantly getting to know new players with the Denver Nuggets. They come and go much faster than I would prefer, but that is the nature of professional basketball. I have noticed that even though our players are tremendously successful as athletes, nearly all of them carry around a list of negatives in their minds. The list may be only four or five thoughts, but it is often harmful to these young athletes. For example, a typical list might read like this: 1) I'm not quite big and strong enough to compete in the NBA. 2) I didn't go to the right college so I don't have good enough credentials entering the league. 3) I'm from a broken home and never had the training growing up that other guys have had so I'm awkward in social situations. 4) I know I don't speak well so I'd better just remain quiet or I'll embarrass myself in front of my teammates. 5) I'm not as handsome as the other guys so I'll just stay to myself as not to be noticed as an ugly duckling.

Some of the things on an individual's negative list may be true, yet some may not be true at all. It really does not matter. The point is, if "tapes" like these are playing over and over in your head, you will eventually believe them, and you will allow them to consume your thoughts. It is harmful and does the opposite in a person's life from the benefit to be gained from Bobb's positive accomplishments list.

Each season I share with the players a story from the Bible illustrating that we are not the first people to formulate negative thoughts about ourselves. From the beginning of time, people have always had lists of "buts" in their minds. "But I'm too short, but I'm too tall, but I'm too old, but I'm too young, but I'm not educated, but I'm this, but I'm that." The "but" list is always available. If we choose to focus on it, it can be a killer. Listen to this dialog between God and Moses, as recorded in

Exodus 3-5. *"The Lord says, 'now I am going to send you to Pharaoh, to demand that he let you lead my people out of Egypt.' 'But I'm not the person for a job like that!' Moses said. Then God told him, 'I will certainly be with you.' 'But,' Moses asked, 'If I go to the people of Israel and tell them that their fathers God has sent me they'll ask which God are you talking about. What shall I tell them?' 'The Sovereign God' was the reply, 'Just say I Am has sent me!' 'But,' Moses said, 'They won't believe me. They won't do what I tell them.' 'What do you have there in your hand?' The Lord asked him. And he replied, ' A shepherd's rod. 'Throw it down on the ground,' the Lord told him, so he did and it became a serpent and Moses ran from it. 'But,' Moses pleaded, 'Oh Lord, I'm just not a good speaker, I never have been.' 'Who makes mouths,' Jehovah asked him 'Isn't it I the Lord.' 'But,' Moses said, 'Please send someone else!' Then the Lord became angry!*

I have taken this account from the *Living Bible* which is a paraphrase, but you get the idea. Even with God himself talking to him, Moses was stuck on his list of "buts" and argued with God on what God had in store for him.

Are you that way? Do you sabotage your own success by playing a negative list of "buts" over and over until you finally believe it to be true? Do you let it dominate your life? Those things in your life that aren't pleasing to you can be turned around and used to build up yourself and others when placed in the hands of God. Your messes can be turned into beautiful, life giving fertilizer if given to God. It is your choice to make, and you make it again and again on a daily basis.

I encourage you to make a list and continue to focus on the positive accomplishments in your life. The time has come for all of us to get off our "buts" and become the positive people God intended us to be!

14

Winning New Teammates

Each year there are new players joining the Denver Nuggets. Some are drafted out of college, while others come to the team in trades from other organizations in the NBA. The basketball staff works very diligently to determine what needs the team has and what players might be available to help meet those needs. It is a process that is continually ongoing, year after year, with no let up. As competitive as the league has become, teams need to continue improving just to maintain.

Professional basketball is big business, but as the team chaplain I hate to see players who have become friends come and go so frequently. I am sometimes able to see the guys who have been traded when their new teams come to town, yet it is just not the same. There is a bond that is established between men when Christ is at the core of their relationship. Even though the bond lasts a lifetime, it is sad for me not to spend the quantity and quality time I am used to spending with the players who have become friends and then have had to leave.

More importantly, it is a hardship on the players' families involved when they are traded. Do we sell this house and buy a new one, or do we wait and see what happens next season? Will we find good schools for our children? All kinds of concerns and questions weigh heavily on the minds of the players and their families when it comes to changing teams. I guess I have come to accept it, but you never get used to it. I love the new guys who come in, but I miss my friends who leave.

I teach the players that tastefully "recruiting" new players for God's squad is a vital part of living the Christian life. Matthew 28:19 says, *"Therefore, go and make disciples of all nations, baptizing them in the name of the Father, and of the Son, and of the Holy Spirit."*

This Great Commission, as it is called, instructs us to go "to the people we come in contact with in our lives" and share Christ with them. The Bible says that *"By their fruit you will recognize them."* Matthew 7:16. If we are followers of Christ, we will influence others to follow Him, too. Our lives will bear the fruit of those who come into relationship with Christ because of our influence.

To many of our players and to many of you, sharing Christ with others may seem awkward and intimidating at first. You may be thinking, "Oh no, leave that to Billy Graham and his crusade team—I couldn't do that!" I am not talking about an in your face, door to door campaign. In fact, I do not see that as Christ's example at all! Yes, churches and crusades like Promise Keepers and Billy Graham lead thousands of people to Christ each year. But in these times, more often than not, people receive Jesus after a number of meaningful personal encounters with a Christian friend. This is called "lifestyle evangelism." In other words, someone sees something in you they like and are drawn to. Eventually, you tell them, "It's not me, I'm as much of a mess as the next guy! If there is anything in me that you find attractive, it is Christ and only Christ."

Don Reeverts did just that for me in 1967 when I was a senior at Thomas Jefferson High School in Denver. His friendship moved me slowly into an acceptance of Christ. My friend, Rich Beach, has literally done it hundreds and hundreds of times in his life because "lifestyle evangelism" has become like breathing to him and he is successful at it! I have personally had the privilege of leading quite a few lost people to Christ, and it is truly a blessing when it happens.

I love the way the *Living Bible* phrases it in 1Corinthians 9:22; *"Yes, whatever a person is like, I try to find common ground with him so that he will let me tell him about Christ and Christ may save him."* See, no force there! It is a privilege God has given us to "let our light shine before men" (Matthew 5:16) and draw them to Him. That is why the manner in which we live and conduct our lives is so critical. If we are too pious and isolated, we repel people. If we are too worldly, we become indistinguishable from those we are seeking to help! The balance is what draws people to Christ.

I teach our players that "common ground" is the target. Use common ground such as meals, golf, movies, concerts, children's activities like sports or school plays; i.e., anything that moves us into a relationship with the unsaved world.

And do not think that you have to be or will always be the final link on the chain that leads someone to Christ. Our job as a "link" in the chain of events and encounters that leads someone to Christ is to just love, listen, enjoy, laugh with, and accept them just as they are. (Romans 5:8) In God's precise moment, when the person is ready, they will ask "What do I have to do to become a Christian?" If you have established that "common ground" evangelism is your approach, you will see this happen.

When someone wants to accept Christ, lead them through the following sequence of scriptures. John 3:16 to John 10:10 to Romans 3:23 to Romans 6:23 to Romans 5:8 to 1 Corinthians 15:3-6 to Revelation 3:20 and finally to John 1:12.

This sequence was taught to me years ago by my friends

with Campus Crusade for Christ. The sequence will help you to walk your soon to be new teammate into an understanding of what they are about to do. Then, after they pray to receive Christ as their personal savior, the angels in heaven will sing, and you will rejoice with them that you have played a minor role in God's incredible plan of salvation!

Look for your opportunities to be God's man or woman in every situation and watch how He starts using you to share His story and love with others who might not know!

15

Becoming Champions

The most wonderful person I have ever met is my wife, Gari. We have been married for 30 years, and no one has meant more to me than she has. My parents, brother, sister, children, and friends have all enriched my life in countless ways, but she is my partner for life. As much as I loved her and learned from her in those early years of marriage, it got even better on September 7, 1988 when she had sinus surgery. The next day she told me, "They had done something to her that wasn't right." The surgery was successful, as she has had no more sinus problems, but she has said ever since that time, that her "brain just doesn't feel right."

It has been 12 years now, and we have tried everything from the Mayo Clinic to the Minrith Meyer Clinic to medication to help her get better. The doctors have treated her for a chemical imbalance caused by surgery, and if you met her today, you would think she was in perfect health. She is beautiful both inside and out but will tell you privately that she is only 70 percent normal and never feels "right." Her courage to go on living and serving our family has been a constant source of inspiration. I respect and adore her beyond words and pray that someday she will be fully healed. I will always view her as one of life's great champions as I watch her persevere and continually focus on Christ. She is a grandmother now, still a great mom, a successful consultant with Masterplanning Group

International, but most of all a Christian woman who has never wavered in her faith and love for Christ. When trouble hits, you can either rebel or surrender to God. She has surrendered to Christ and lives daily as a testimony to His love and healing power.

As important as it is to *do* our jobs well, *"working for the Lord and not for men,"* Colossians 3:23, it is more important to *live* our entire lives well. I encourage our players to strive to win the NBA championship, but strive even more to *be* champions in life! 2 Timothy 2:1-5 says, *"You then, my son, be strong in the grace that is in Christ Jesus. And the things you have heard me say in the presence of many witnesses entrust to reliable men who will also be qualified to teach others. Endure hardship with us like a good soldier of Christ Jesus. No one serving as a soldier gets involved in civilian affairs—he wants to please his commanding officer. Similarly, if anyone competes as an athlete, he does not receive the victor's crown unless he competes according to the rules."*

The word champion literally means "compete." We are called to compete as Christians by defeating anything that tries to pull us down and compete in the power of God. My wife competes every day for her health. She wants to feel better, and she does, but it is a continuing battle. In the midst of the ongoing battle, however, she is already a champion!

I let the players know that this championship of life is like no other. As grand as a NBA championship ring might be, how about the reward that is ours someday in heaven when we meet Christ face to face? However, if we are to be champions, we must press on with relentless intensity toward the goal of becoming like Christ in our character. We are literally "contending" for the high prize by doing our part in the Body of Christ to insure victory for the whole team!

In John 15:5 Jesus says, *"Without me, you can do nothing."* The key, then, is to acknowledge that it is in, through, and by the authority and power of Jesus that we strive to win the championship. It is in His power that we prepare ourselves to confront and overcome opponents. Health problems, poor relationships, financial struggles, career disappointments? Whatever the world wants to throw at us, in His power we need to persevere and win because, *"I can do all things through Christ who strengthens me."* Philippians 4:13.

My wife has tried everything known to man to feel 100 percent well. She has gone way beyond just doing her best. Because of this, she is now healthier, happier, and closer to a complete healing than she has been in years. A half-hearted effort would have left her too ill to function. Many would have given up, but she has an inner strength in Christ that drives her to get well for her own sake, and for the sake of her family and God.

Every champion has this same drive. You know the people I am talking about—you may even be one of them yourself.

Therefore, you must decide to what extent you are willing to go to live your life as God's champion. Will you become a champion in a world full of quitters? Will you strive for the top prize in Christ or settle for mediocrity in terms of who you are? It is time to decide, and it is time to move out! Let's join together and press onward and upward in our lives as we cast aside anything that would hold us back!

16

Light It Up!

During the course of a basketball game when a player is scoring from all over the court at will, he is said to be "lighting it up." It is a common phrase among the coaches and players in the NBA and has been for years. I use this phrase to help introduce what has become a favorite topic at chapel for many of our players.

I set the stage by turning out all of the lights in our chapel room at the Pepsi Center in Denver. I am careful to make sure each player is settled before I do this, because the room becomes almost completely black, and I do not want a player stumbling or injuring himself because of my antics! There is usually some mumbling about "what is Bo up to," but the veterans on the team know what to expect and encourage me to go on.

I begin by talking about the darkness. I remind them of the fact that fear and evil are commonly associated with darkness. I ask them what they associate with the darkness. As an example, were they afraid as children when the lights were turned off?

Then, after a few minutes our eyes begin to adjust to the darkness. I warn them that if we, as Christians, persist on a path of embracing the darkness of this world, we soon become used to the darkness. Our flirtation with the world then causes us to be ineffective in our attempts to reach others with the

Gospel of Christ. I share with the players how easy it is for us to adjust to darkness rather than choosing the light of Christ. In John 3:19-21 the Bible says, *"This is the verdict; Light has come into the world, but men loved darkness instead of light because their deeds were evil. Everyone who does evil hates the light, and will not come into the light for fear that his deeds will be exposed. But whoever lives by the truth comes into the light so that it may be seen plainly that what he has done has been done through God."* 1 Corinthians 3:13 says that, *"His work will be shown for what it is, because The Day will bring it to light."* The fact is that in darkness, many things can be hidden. Light will expose who we are, and Jesus Christ refers to Himself in John 8:12 as *"The Light of the World."* 1 John 1:5 says that *"God is light and in Him is no darkness at all."*

At this point, I light a candle that is sitting on a table in the center of the room. The light from the candle is very bright, and I ask each guy to focus on the candle and think about Jesus as the light of the world. He penetrates all darkness, just like the candle does our room. He exposes every part of the darkness that has been previously hidden. His light is the illumination we need to avoid the traps the dark world has set before us. By keeping our eyes fixed on the light of Christ, we make our way through a world that is getting darker by the minute!

Try other ways if you will, but eventually, even if you have adjusted to the darkness, you will cry out for the life available to you in the light of Christ!

The Bible teaches that when we commit our lives to a faithful relationship with Christ and live in obedience, we become like Him as a light in this world! Matthew 5:14-16 says, *"You are the light of the world. A city on a hill cannot be hidden. Neither do people light a lamp and put it under a bowl. Just as they put it on its stand, and it gives light to everyone in the home. In the same way, let your light shine before man, that they see your good deeds, and praise your Father in heaven."* Wow! We are to be light in this dark world as we represent Jesus Christ! What greater challenge and calling could there be in life than living as light to everyone we meet? I challenge our players as they continue to stare at that light to think about how they are doing in this area of their lives. Do they take seriously these words of Christ when He tells us that, "we are the light of the world."

Finally, I end by warning them not to be teammates with the darkness. 2 Corinthians 6:14 says, *"Do not be yoked together with unbelievers. For what do righteousness and worldliness have in common? Or what fellowship can light have with darkness?"* As a light in the world, we can reach out and minister to those in darkness, but avoid being "yoked." Avoid being linked in partnerships, friendships, or situations that might cause you to make decisions based on anything other than God's instructions.

Continuing to be light can be one of the most difficult areas of walking with Christ. Why? Because we live in earthly darkness and are surrounded by its presence. Therefore, the challenge becomes staying true to Christ and all His ways, and continuously living as a light in the darkness wherever you are today and wherever God leads you in the future!

17

Uniform of Faith

In the summer of 1971, I had just signed a professional base-ball contract with the St. Louis Cardinals. The next spring I reported to the minor league complex in St. Petersburg, Florida for spring training. I was impressed that even as minor lea-guers, we were wearing the big league uniforms with the famous logo that the Cardinals had always worn. Almost every day, I thought to myself as I got suited up—Stan Musial, Lou Brock, and Bob Gibson wore this same kind of uniform! When I put on my uniform, I was reminded how my dad had always taught me to respect the fact that God had given me the talent to be an athlete and never to take it for granted.

Each year that I have been chaplain for the Nuggets, I have reminded the guys of the honor it is to wear the Denver Nuggets NBA uniform. Most of them know it and appreciate it, but once in a while, I have encountered a rookie who appears to take it for granted. Usually, they do not last too long with this kind of attitude. However, the great players seem to sense how truly special it is to play the game. I ask them to take just a split second every night when they suit up to say a spe-cial thanks to God for giving them the talent, and to the Nuggets organization for giving them the opportunity to play in the NBA.

As wonderful as it is to be an athlete at any level and rep-resent your school or city, how much more wonderful it is to be called a child of God! Once we receive Christ as our Lord and Savior we become his child, and that title and privilege should mean more than anything else in our lives. *"How great is the love the Father has lavished on us, that we should be called children of God."* 1 John 3:1

At chapel every year, I suggest to the guys that putting on the uniform of Faith every day is their highest honor. I also encourage them that in order to accomplish all God wants them to in their lifetime requires the full armor of God.

The "world" will continually attack us from all directions. Land mines are carefully placed in our paths to destroy us. Knowing that we face challenges daily that can injure us, it is a <u>must</u> that we never leave the door of our homes without the Uniform of Faith protecting us in every way!

"Therefore put on the whole armor of God, so that when the day of evil comes, you may be able to stand your ground, and after you have done everything, to stand." Ephesians 6:13

The Armor of God–
Helmet of Salvation -

To protect our minds
Thank Him for your salvation
Pray for the salvation of others

Breastplate of Righteousness -

To protect our emotions
Phil 3:9 – "and be found in Him, not having a righteousness of my own that comes from the law, but that which is

through faith in Christ
The righteousness that comes
from God and is by faith."

Belt of Truth -

Pray to live Truth, seek Truth,
speak Truth—Jesus is the
Truth

Shod Your Feet with the Gospel of Peace –

Pray to bring God into every
situation of your day—go
where He wants you to go and
do what He wants you to do –
share the gospel

Taking up the Sword of the Spirit –

Which is the word of God. See
Heb. 4:12

Shield of Faith –

With which you can extinguish
all the flaming arrows of the
evil one. Activate your faith
against all the events that come
against you—know that you
are protected by God

My son, Andy, overcame great challenges to win a schol-
arship to the University of Colorado and perform as the starting punter for three years. I will never forget the first time I saw
him in his CU uniform. Because I was so proud of him and all

that he had already accomplished in his life, I had to turn and walk away for a moment to compose myself. I greeted him on the practice field with tears still in my eyes because I could not contain the joy I felt for him. He looked great in that Colorado uniform!

How much more emotion does God and every angel in heaven have for you the first time you suit up in your Uniform of Faith? When you dress out in the full armor of God and take to this field called life, He must weep with joy, too, at the sight of you! Doesn't that thought make you want to represent Christ in a worthy way? He knows you completely and loves you and calls you to be a member of His glorious team! Living for Him is the most successful life available to anyone!

18

Teammates for Life

On one of the road trips I took with the Nuggets, the hotel where we were staying had a great swimming pool and hot tub area. The team did not play until the next day, so upon arrival, some players said to me, "Meet us in the hot tub—we want to hear your life story."

We had known each other for the entire season, yet what I heard these guys saying was, "Let's get to know each other at a deeper level." I appreciated the time we spent together that night just sharing all kinds of things about our lives. Only one of the players who joined us in the hot tub is still with the Nuggets. Others remain in the League (5 years later) and only one is completely out of basketball. Even though we are scattered at this point, we all remain friends, and I believe those friendships will last a lifetime.

It has been said that true happiness cannot exist for men and women without friendship. Ecclesiastes 4:10 says, *"Woe to him who is alone, for when he falls, he has no one to lift him."* There is tremendous pleasure in knowing you have a friend that you can speak to man to man, woman to woman, friend to friend.

Every season, I present at least one chapel on friendship. I share some scriptures pertaining to friendship, but mostly I ask the players to consider a more concentrated effort on reaching out to their teammates as friends. Character and talent will win championships, but the chemistry of a team is just as important. I believe chemistry is built through the love that comes from being friends with your teammates.

There have been seasons when it does not seem like many of our guys are friends, but instead are enemies. During those times, I ask the Christian leaders of our team to step forward, take initiative, and strive to build friendships. I share with them about my daughter Ashley, and how she desperately wanted to have just one friend when she was in the third grade, because she was so lonely. She and my wife, Gari, would pray every night for God to give her just one friend. Finally, in the fourth grade at a new school, God blessed her with some wonderful friends, and she continues now as a wife and mother to place a high value on her friendships. Why is she so successful at friendships? She worked at it because it was, and still is, very important to her. She learned that if you want to have more friends, then you must learn to be a better friend.

Sometimes the guys respond to working on friendships and I can see some improvement in the friendships and the chemistry of the team. But some times, it is just too forced because there is not enough "common ground" to build a friendship. It is at those times that God can step in and do his miraculous work!

I share with the players that the accountability dimension of friendship can be difficult, especially with men. To be accountable to a friend means to "submit to another person's judgement or authority." The message being sent here is "I need you!" Too often, men feel that they are exhibiting a weakness by saying to anyone, "I need you." Ashley and I struggled in our relationship as father and daughter because I was often times too controlling and overpowering. She is very much like me and would have no part of my controlling behavior. But then during one of the most stressful times of my life, I needed her help like never before, and she could feel it. Undeniably, I would not have survived the ordeal I was experiencing if she had not helped me. In the fiery furnace of my need, she ministered to me in an all out effort to help me. The result was forging a beautiful friendship with my grown daughter that will last for a lifetime.

The risk of being known and accepted by a close friend is another reason all of us hesitate to enter into deep friendships. Many of us have been burned by a friend's inability to hold a confidence, but that should not keep us from trying. Regular fellowship with close friends can become as important to us as anything on our schedules, but it does take time and require effort.

I encourage the Nuggets players not to miss the opportunity to build some life-long friendships during their days as NBA players. I encourage them to invest the time and emotional energy in the lives of a handful of friends that will become as close as family members. The rewards far surpass the investments and I encourage you to pursue close friendships as one of the great blessings of life!

19

The Ladder of Love

NBA players are no different than the rest of us when it comes to trying to determine their priorities in life. I have seen rookies come into the league and get so caught up in all of the activity and demands placed on them that they never seem to reach their full potential as players. On any given night during the regular season, a player may have to arrange for his family tickets to be left at the "will call" window to be picked up, do a special interview for one of the local papers, TV stations, or radio stations, or meet with someone special who has request-ed a quick "meet and greet." This is all before he actually enters the locker room to begin focusing and preparing for the game. Once in the locker room, he will have the options of a light work out with weights or the stationary bike, treatment on some ailment from the trainer, getting his ankles taped, warm-ing up with a coach on the court, and finally getting the "game plan" for that night's opponent. All of these potential demands can be very time consuming and confusing.

In an effort to assist the players with this confusion, I try to present once a year, a chapel service on "God's Order of Priorities." In Matthew 22:37-40, Jesus says, *"Love the Lord your God with all your heart and with all your soul and with all your mind. This is the first and greatest commandment and the second is like it: Love your neighbor as yourself. All the Law and the prophets hang on the two commandments."*

Over twenty years ago, my wife Gari and I were involved with the formation of an organization that presented marriage retreats. During the development phase of our organization, our dear friends and co-workers, Helen and Everett Dye helped us create a tool that we called The Ladder of Love. It was Helen's idea that led to the concept of a simple ladder that looked like the one below: We call it "The Ladder of Love"

Christ
Self
Family
Friends
Fellowman

The Ladder of Love is an illustration of God's order of priorities which is carefully listed in the book of Matthew. The top rung is our relationship with Christ. If the top rung is not in "good shape," then the ones below it will suffer. He is the one who teaches us how to unconditionally love others. If the rung of our love for our "self" is not balanced and healthy, we will not have enough to offer the three rungs below. Under family, we taught that our "horizontal" relationships (i.e. our wives and husbands) come first, then our children, and then other members of our immediate families. Friends and then fellowman follow as areas of priority before we even start to give consideration to our daily tasks and responsibilities. If we want to please God with our lives, then we should focus on looking at our relationships with this "grid" which is composed of the rungs of this ladder.

When I share this information at chapel, I ask the players to consider how much time they normally spend studying the Bible. I then ask them to compare that to the amount of time they would normally spend reading the sports page or watching TV. Not surprisingly, for all of us, the time allocation was weighted heavily towards almost all alternative areas other than the study of the Bible. I then share how convenient it is for us that He gave us a "Cliff Notes" version of how to follow the Bible in Matthew 22. At a minimum, we should at least be able to live according to His challenge in these verses to focus on relationships.

I then challenge them with this idea of living with a focus on their own, personal Ladders of Love! Would they, at a minimum, ask themselves each and every day if their top priority is to live their lives according to God's instructions in Matthew 22:37-40. They all agree it is at least worth a try!

My friend Bob Beltz teaches that the world typically instructs us to use people and love "things." But what we really should do is love people and use the things of this world to love them even more. Our goal should be to allow God to show us everything it means to be in a loving relationship with Him, and then from that foundation, love ourselves and others in ways that only He can teach! In Bob's words—love people and use things! That's the way God designed it, and The Ladder of Love can help you to remember to live your life that way everyday!

How simple does God have to make it for us all to give it a try? Focus on relationships, starting with Christ, and see what happens in your life. Live for Him, and not the "desires of the flesh" that can be found in the world. It may be surprising to you to see how simple it all can be.

20

Tragedy

On April 20, 1999 at about 11:00 a.m. a tragedy occurred at
Columbine High School in Denver, Colorado. Throughout
that day, we continued to learn more of the details about what
had actually happened. By 4:30 p.m. when I arrived at
McNichols Arena for our home game against Portland, basketball was the last thing on anyone's mind. I was immediately ushered into the team president's office and asked my opin-
ion as to what the Nuggets should do as an organization in
response to the tragedy. There were six or seven other people
in the room who were responsible for most of the decisions
that needed to be made, so I stuck to my role as chaplain and
simply said, "Let's gather the staff for prayer, and I'll go to the
locker room and wait to see what the players want to do."
Within twenty minutes, the Portland team bus from their hotel
had arrived at the arena, and one of their players called our
locker room to ask if both teams could get together immediately for a chapel service. I of course said, "Yes," and we con-
vened in a nearby room for chapel. The game had been can-
celled by the time our group got together.

For a short time, we prayed for the victims of the shooting,
their families, and the safety of other students and faculty
members at the school. Soon after, we began a discussion that
I will never forget. About five players were present from each
team, and I asked them if they would know what to say if they

were asked to go to Columbine right then and comfort the families of the victims. I went on to ask, "Would you have any answers for them as to why awful things like this happen?" To a man, they responded by saying, "No way. We'd have no answers and would not want to be asked." My job, at that point, was to, "coach them up."

I had not had much time to think about my own words of comfort if I had been asked to speak to the families. I thought what was most important to explain to the players at that point was why I thought evil things like the Columbine tragedy happened almost everyday throughout the world.

To begin with, when Adam and Eve looked at God in the Garden of Eden and basically said, "We want to run our own lives, so pass the apples," we were all set on a course that includes pain, problems and trouble. This is referred to as "the fall of man." It is at this turning point that sin and all kinds of evil became a part of our lives. I went on to explain to our players that men and women today, most without even knowing it, are still looking God in the eye and defying Him when they choose to go their own ways, and in effect, disregard His truth. The two young men who committed the murders at Columbine were going down a path that was not what God intended for them. Obviously, they did not receive their life shaping and life changing information from the Bible. I would guess that they had gone to the TV set, local video games, the Internet, music, or their friends to get their beliefs and values. Then, with the "truth" they believed, which was confirmed by the small group of friends they belonged to, they decided the proper response or action to that "truth" was to kill and wound their classmates.

Unfortunately, evil acts like Columbine will probably happen more and more because of the condition of men's hearts. It is very sad and tragic for all of us, that men and women do not seek a relationship with Jesus Christ and a commitment to obey his instructions in the scriptures.

I would like to state here that I am nothing more than a fellow pilgrim on the journey of life. I am a sinner who makes as many mistakes as the next guy and is constantly falling short of who God would want me to be. I am also a Christian who has the intent daily to live a life of obedience to Jesus Christ and the instructions of the Holy Scripture. The key to avoiding tragedies like Columbine is to be Christ oriented, not oriented to the evils of this world.

At some point in my sharing, one of the Portland players asked me if he could say a word or two. He said, "I know what you're talking about because my grandmother taught me how to live as a Christian. Since I got in the NBA, however, I've drifted into a way of life that is wrong and I know it. Because of what happened today, I'm going to change and go back to what I know is right!" I was proud of him for his boldness and transparency. We occasionally talk, and he is still on track.

Just as awful as Columbine is the fact that millions of people neglect or reject a relationship with a God who loves us completely and unconditionally and Who's word has the perfect answer to every question and situation that comes our way. At a minimum, it seems that we should put forth an all out effort to make this a better and a safer place to live. We should seek goodness, safety, health, and love for every person. To do this, we must live in the power of the Holy Spirit, and not in the grip of a dark and hateful world. Tragedies will continue to happen, but triumph awaits for those choosing Christ.

21

The Blame Game

"Up to a point a man's life is shaped by environment, heredity, and movements and changes in the world about him. Then there comes a time when it lies within his grasp to shape the clay of his life into the sort of thing he wishes to be. Only the weak blame parents, their race, their times, lack of good fortune, or the quirks of fate. Everyone has it within his power to say, *This I am today; that I will be tomorrow.*"

The Walking Dream
Louis L'Amour

When I first read this quote, it struck me how right Louis L'Amour was. There is this weakness of not taking responsibility that is becoming more common among people today. Too often it seems people want to blame others when things go wrong. We all have friends who have never once said, "I was wrong—that was my fault!" Isn't that amazing? Imagine the pressure they have placed on themselves to be perfect. These are people who never think of themselves as making a mistake or being at fault, much less apologizing. Consequently, they have set a pattern of placing the blame elsewhere for what should be their own responsibility.

Character must be one of the key components of an NBA team. Without it, no amount of talent or coaching is enough to consistently win the big games. One aspect of character that is especially critical on a basketball team is the desire and willingness of the players to own up to and accept their portion of the blame when something does go wrong with the team.

During the course of one season in Denver, I began to notice a pattern with one player on our team. When we won, he was quoted in the papers as saying, "*We* did this or *we* did that"—it was a "team" thing, which was at least better than taking all the credit for the victory himself. When we lost, however, he was continually quoted as saying, "I don't know what *they* were thinking or I don't know why *they* weren't better." The "we" went away and the blame went to "they." It got to the point where this pattern effected everyone in the organization and became counter productive for the team.

The Bible teaches that pride is one reason we cannot admit our fault. In 1 Corinthians 8:2, the *Living Bible* paraphrase says, *"If anyone thinks he knows all the answers, he is just showing his ignorance."* Possibly the two greatest verses in scripture pertaining to the fact that we are all wrong from time to time are in Romans 3:23 which says, *"All have sinned and fall short of the glory of God"* and 1 John 1:8,10 which says, *"If we claim to be without sin, we deceive ourselves and the truth is not in us. If we claim we have not sinned, we make him out to be a liar and his word has no place in our lives."* It takes only one ounce of humility to respond to these scriptures by simply saying, "Yes, you are right God, include me when you say *all*, because I have been wrong and have sinned." It is the height of ignorance and arrogance to not recognize God's truth about how we are *all* wrong at times and we need to ask for the forgiveness of God and others.

However, there are times when things go wrong, and no one is at fault, but we still insist on blaming someone else for the problem. For instance, we all have been lost on a road trip with our families and instead of turning the car around, going back and asking for directions, we blame it on something or someone else. We think or say things like, "That road sign was marked incorrectly," or "She told me the wrong way." For whatever reasons, we have become a society that finds some warped satisfaction in blaming people or circumstances when problems happen, even though no one or thing is at fault!

I encourage our team each season not to fall into the habit of blaming God, people, circumstances, or anything else for what is happening when it is their own fault. The "victim" and "poor me" spirit pulls others down as individuals and as a team. Strong people are comfortable with who they are and saying, "I blame no one—this one is on me. I take responsibility." God responds to those cries of confession. 1 John 1:9 says, *"If we confess our sins, He is faithful and just and will forgive us our sins and purify us from unrighteousness."* He died on the cross for this purpose and wants us to respond by confessing it to Him and to others when we blow it.

In the August 12, 1991, issue of *Time* magazine, the cover story was "Busybodies and Crybabies—What's happening to the American Character?" The article stated, "A society can't operate if everyone has rights and no one has responsibilities." Therefore, as God's men and women, it should be our daily goal to serve God and others in love. We know we are frail and flawed, so we must go into each day knowing that we are probably going to blow it in some way.

With this in mind, we must accept the responsibility when it is our fault and say, "I was wrong and I'm sorry."

It is pleasing to God and is the right thing for us to do. By resisting the temptation to blame others, we exhibit a maturity in Christ that is pleasing to everyone we touch with our lives!

22

Keeping Score

Because I played college and professional athletics, my family and friends made the assumption that I would want our first child to be a boy. Instead, when Gari was pregnant in 1972 and I was still playing pro baseball, I began to pray that our baby would be a girl because that's what I truly wanted. In those days, it was not common to find out the sex of a baby ahead of time, so I just kept praying and on October 20, 1972 our daughter Ashley was born! I also prayed specifically for a blonde, and perhaps overdid it because her hair was almost white for the first 10 years of her life!

My prayers are not always answered like this, but in this case, I got just what I had been asking God for. Ashley was 100% all girl from day one. She wore *only* dresses as play clothes. She was into bride books from the time she was four, and she announced to her mother and me that she was "a party girl" and could not sleep as long as we had guests in our home! She was the most beautiful little girl in the world and I could not have been more proud of her. Today, she is happily married to Andy Larson, and has a beautiful baby girl named Mackensie. She and Lars (Andy's nickname) have a wonderful marriage and I am proud of her and thankful that Gari and I are so blessed with a daughter like Ashley.

Our son, Andy, came along on April 15, 1974. I have always said that Andy's birth balanced out the pain of paying taxes on that day every year! Andy was 100% all boy from day one. He put on a full Cleveland Indians baseball uniform at age four because his Granddad had played for the Indians from 1946 through 1956. He looked so cute in it, but the problem was he refused to take it off for about four years! Every day, week after week, unless we went to war over it, he had on the same socks, pants, jersey and cap! Gari hardly had time to wash the uniform to get it ready for the next day.

When Andy turned six, he and I started a Saturday morning ritual that lasted for years. We would walk to a par three golf course near us and play together one or two 9-hole rounds of golf. Andy was very competitive. He would write down the score after every hole and on the occasions when he would make a par, he would point out to me that, " I made a three, and you made a four, Dad." If his score was not up to his expectations, he would get angry! After observing this for a few weeks, I said to Andy one Saturday morning, "How about today we don't keep score. Let's just enjoy the sunshine and the fact that we're together and not keep track of how we're playing." I'll never forget what he said to me when with surprise in his eyes, he exclaimed, "Not keep *score!* Why would we even *play* if we're not going to keep score?" His shock made me realize that even as a little boy, he was a fierce competitor and wanted to know by his score how he was doing.

Andy went on to play college football at the University of Colorado. As he was standing in punt formation ready to kick the ball at Michigan Stadium or against Notre Dame in the Fiesta Bowl, I would think to myself, "He's still keeping score—he wants to kick this ball as far as he can to help C.U. win!"

Andy and his wife Dana have been married for two years

and I am so proud of who they both are as God's people. The lessons he and Ashley taught me about life are still fresh in my mind every day, and I use them often as illustrations for my chapel services.

Being in relationship with the competitive men that I come to know every year in chapel is a real blessing. I try to think about them as little guys like Andy was, and I can imagine every one of them looking at their own dads saying, "Not keep score, are you crazy?" I guess it is part of human nature. We want to know how we are stacking up against others. Am I doing okay or am I falling behind? If it can be measured, then we want to measure it. But, God's love for us cannot be measured. Ephesians 2:8 says, *"For it is by grace you have been saved, through faith—and this not from yourselves, it is the gift of God—not by works—so that no one can boast."*

I think believing that we are saved by God's grace and not by our own accomplishments is hard for some people to accept, especially competitive people. We say, "God has given me a gift, and all I have to do is accept it? Come on, let me *do* something to earn it. Let me *strive*, and *accomplish* something before I'm entitled to my gift, *especially* a gift this great!" It is common for men and women to place value on what can be earned, and think, "If I can't earn it then it's not worth much."

A lot of this thinking can be attributed to ego. The truth is you cannot keep score as to how you are doing with God. You cannot *earn* God's love or his favor. It does not work that way. God's love for you is perfect, and He loves you the same on your best day or on your worst. His love never changes, and all he asks of us is to accept this free gift.

Do not fall into the trap of thinking "Well, I've done this or that, thinking better of yourself than you are, with an attitude that God is wise to pick me as his own, the scoreboard tells the story—I win!" Conversely, do not think less of yourself than you are and say to yourself, "I'm a mess and don't deserve God's love—the scoreboard shows me as a total zero, why would God want me?"

God does want you to see yourself as He sees you. His arms are open wide to you when you reach out and receive His gift through faith.

Grace by definition means unmerited favor. There is no scoreboard for grace! You cannot win or lose God's love! Therefore, when it comes to God, if you live your life by a scoreboard, it will always be a hindrance to you. Accept that if you have faith enough to humbly receive His gift, you will always win the most important victory of your life!

23

Knowing Your Opponent

Every night when I enter the Denver Nuggets locker room at the Pepsi Center to greet the players and prepare for chapel, I realize we have one of the most beautiful and spacious facilities in the NBA. The individual lockers are huge with comfortable black reclining chairs in front of each one of them. In the center of the room is a giant Nuggets logo. The entire length of the wall opposite the players' lockers consists of two giant dry erase boards and a big screen television. On the TV set there is a tape being played of the opponents last game. The NBA directs a cooperative effort of teams sharing their tapes with each other. The players are instructed to arrive at the arena no later than 5:30 p.m. for a game that will start at 7:05 p.m. The coach usually begins his pre-game talk at 6:40 p.m. At some point between 5:30 and 6:40, as the guys are suiting up, they will watch the scouting tape on the TV. They concentrate on who they will be guarding that night or who will be guarding them. They look for any little thing that could give them an edge. They also look for any little tendency that they should be aware of in terms of causing them a problem on either offense or defense.

The assistant coaches have carefully filled in the two boards on either side of the TV with diagrams of defensive and offensive sets that will be used against that night's specific opponent. The coaches then review with the team during the pre-game talk these game sets. They will also discuss specific players on the other team and what our guys should do to get themselves ready. It is a continuous analysis of the opponent and begins weeks before the night of the game when Denver's scouts are on the road watching the opponents. These scouts report back to the coaches what the opponent is looking like at that particular point in the season.

In chapel each year, I make sure that our players know without a doubt that as Christians we face a minimum of two worthy opponents every day of our lives; Satan and the world. The Bible warns us to, *"Be self-controlled and alert. Your enemy the devil prowls around like a roaring lion looking for someone to devour. Resist him, standing firm in the faith, because you know that your brothers throughout the world are undergoing the same kind of sufferings."* 1 Peter 5:8-9. It does not say that Satan wants to *distract us* or *discourage us.* It says he wants to *devour us!* He attacks us at the point of our weakness and entices us to drift away from God and the things of His kingdom. He is constantly laying traps and land mines in our paths in an effort to ruin anything and everything that God has built into us, through Christ. To underestimate *this* opponent would be a foolish mistake!

The second opponent is the world and all of its attractions. 1 John 2:15 says, *"Do not love the world or anything in the world. If anyone loves the world, the love of the Father is not in him. For everything in the world—the cravings of sinful man, the lust of his eyes, and the boasting of what he has and does—comes not from the Father, but from the world. The world and its desires pass away, but the man who does the will of God lives forever."* This scripture refers to losing our first love for God, and becoming "lukewarm" towards Him. (Revelation 3:15-16) An attraction to the world and the things of the world slowly pulls us from the

Father. He blesses us with material gain in the *spirit*, and then we respond by acting as if we did it ourselves and turn it into an act of the *flesh* that eventually pushes us deeper into worldliness and away from holiness. To push the world back into balance and to resist Satan, we must concentrate daily on drawing nearer to Christ!

Where are you today in your life? Do you consciously prepare to do battle with Satan and the world? Do you let the two have their way with you as you slowly drift further and further from Jesus? It is critical to our lives as Christians that we keep our eyes fixed on Jesus and not Satan. To go blindly on as if the opponent was not out to devour us is unwise. I encourage you to stay strong in the Lord and defeat the enemy at every point of attack through fellowship with other Christians, consistent prayer, and daily interaction with the Bible.

24

Drifting into Bad Habits

In the nine seasons I have been with the Denver Nuggets, I have been fortunate to meet and become friends with some of the best coaches in the NBA. The Nuggets have had five different head coaches during my time and at least a dozen assistants in those seasons. Without exception, they are all great guys and very good at what they do.

Coaches work for hours with the players on things that help players reach their full potential as athletes. It is the coach's job to notice any bad habits that the players may have slipped into unintentionally. The sooner a coach notices, the better the chance of them being corrected without hurting the player or the team.

Bad habits can be described as anything the player is doing on the court that is fundamentally unsound. Bad habits give an individual a potential problem in being his best at every aspect of his game. Bad habits can ruin careers or, in the broader perspective, even lives if they are not identified quickly and corrected.

Great players welcome the advice and input offered by their coaches. The great coaches see things sooner and more completely than others. They offer help to their players to eliminate bad habits and help them to play the game fundamentally sound. The likelihood of victory is enhanced when players and coaches are working together to eliminate bad habits.

I alert our players at chapel each season to what the book of Hebrews refers to as "the drift of the world." Hebrews 1:2 says, *"We must pay more careful attention, therefore, to what we have heard, so that we do not drift away."* Upon reading this you may ask, what is it that "we have heard?" The answer is the salvation story of Jesus and His resurrection. Why should we pay careful attention? Because nothing you will hear is more important and life changing than this message. Why then would we drift from Christ? Because bad habits cause us to drift. These bad habits form slowly and unintentionally over time—like the drift of a vessel on the water, pulling us away from Christ and His best for us.

Because I am asked by the Nuggets organization to serve in the leadership role of chaplain, it is my duty to observe and instruct when necessary in the spiritual arena. Therefore, I want the players to clearly understand how "drifting" is dangerous business.

There are many people, including many NBA players, who were raised "in the church" and can recall the moment when they received Christ. They can recall times of joy, peace, and calm in their lives because of their relationship with Jesus. Yet, for one reason or another, some of them have drifted away from God. They quit "paying close attention to what they had heard" and started listening to other voices, being pulled away from Christ and into the worldliness of their lives.

One player who is probably the best friend I have made in my time with the Nuggets drifted into sexual sin. Other guys were sleeping with anybody and everybody so why shouldn't he? It is never usually a quick sprint to sin but just a slow step at a time—drifting. When my friend realized the danger and sin he was in, he identified the "habit" he had formed, confessed it to me and more importantly to his wife, turned away from his "habit" and within weeks was back on the path with Christ. But, there was deep pain inflicted on his wife by his actions, and only her love for Christ gave her the ability to forgive him and give their marriage a fresh start.

He and his wife publicly speak on this subject today to help others who suffer from the sin of infidelity. They now have one of the strongest marriages you could imagine and are tremendous parents! He knew he almost missed out entirely on God's blessing for his life by drifting into his bad "habit." Because he turned away from his bad habit, today he is a man focused on living for Christ, and God has blessed him abundantly!

Others gradually drift into pornography, debt, and other sins that take them away from God. I do not sit in judgement because I have done my share of drifting, but I do alert people to the fact that drifting is dangerous and can be stopped. Constant prayer, Bible study, and fellowship with other Christians are keys to turning in a new direction.

Protect your mind and heart from the potential of drifting by "paying careful attention to what you have heard!" Your relationship with Christ is too wonderful and beautiful to allow anything to get in your way. Stay strong in Christ and paddle upstream against the bad currents of this world!

25

Pine Time

Who knows when or where it started, but athletes in almost every sport have always referred to sitting on the bench as "riding the pine." I have ridden the pine before, and it is no fun. As an athlete, you want to be in the middle of the action. Players hate sitting on the sidelines waiting and wondering if they will get the chance to play. Often times you are on the pine because of an injury. Other times it may be because someone took your position by playing better. Some players even get sideways with the coach and wind up watching. I was late for basketball practice once in high school, and Coach Gaston Santi decided I would learn my lesson by watching the first quarter next to him on the bench. I mouthed off once to Sox Walseth, my college basketball coach, during his halftime speech and never left his side the rest of the night! I did not like it, but I learned my lessons.

"Riding the pine" is actually a part of athletics because someone has to sit! It is impossible for every player on the team to be in the game at the same time. The rules do not allow that many participants. However, it is never fun to "ride the pine."

In 1992 I was a part of a group of guys that got into a huge legal mess in Denver. The details are too extensive and involved to share here, but suffice to say, I had been stupid and negligent in my business affairs and the consequences were devastating for me and my family. We were honest and forthright in how we handled the situation but got crushed in the process. I share this to say that before God and men, I felt like the appropriate action for me to take as a Christian was to resign every leadership position I held at the time. It was painful to step down from our church staff, my position on the Promise Keepers board, and others, but they were the right steps to take. I felt for the first time in my life that I was on the sidelines permanently, "riding the pine," because of the mess I had helped to create.

There are so many people who feel the same way I felt. Frustrated Christians wonder why God has them watching instead of participating. Some feel that they are on the pine because they are too old or maybe too young. Others, like in my case, made a mistake and do not feel worthy. Still others do not feel they have anything to offer and sit for years in a posture of paralysis. Looking back, I see a number of reasons why it was helpful to sit and watch for a while, both in athletics and in life. Being disciplined was never fun, even though I needed it to grow.

There are a few aspects of discipline I will share with my players. First there are times that our loving Father disciplines us for our own good. Hebrews 12:7-11 says, *"Endure hardship as discipline; God is treating you as sons. For what son is not disciplined by his father? If you are not disciplined (and everyone undergoes discipline), then you are illegitimate children and not true sons. Moreover, we have all had human fathers who disciplined us and we respected them for it. How much more should we submit to the Father of our spirits and live! Our fathers disciplined us for a little while as they thought best; but God disciplines us for our good, that we may share in his holiness. No discipline seems pleasant at the time, but painful. Later on, however, it produces a harvest of right-eousness and peace for those who have been trained by it."*

If we truly do "submit to the Father of our spirits" we will not grumble so loudly or as often during our times on the pine. If we see ourselves as students in God's classroom and not victims, we will understand that no matter how things look or might feel, God is in control and His timing is perfect! He will bring us off the bench and back into the game when we mature in Him and are ready to glorify Him and not ourselves!

Secondly, if God is preparing us for some higher calling or service, He sometimes allows things to come into our lives to bench us for a while. In Luke 22:31, Jesus says, *"Simon, Simon, Satan has asked to sift you as wheat."* The process of sifting is one in which the chaff is separated from the wheat. The chaff is the worthless outer covering of the wheat. This process separates the good from the bad, leaving only the good. What Jesus is saying is that we too will be sifted. He also says that Satan *asked* for permission. The point is, we are protected by Jesus, and Satan does not have a free reign on our lives. We belong to Jesus, so even during a time of sifting, we can know for certain that Jesus is in control! He controls the intensity, the duration, and the method of sifting.

If you are on the bench and wonder why, it may simply be your time of sifting! When the sifting is complete, if you have focused on Christ, you will have grown closer to Him and who He wants you to be as His man or woman. Then you will be ready to be used in ways you could never imagine.

I am a much better man today for what I went through in 1992. I am also much closer to Christ, my family, and my friends than I was before. God has brought me off the bench and is using me now in ways I never dreamed possible. He loved me enough to help me get ready!

I encourage our players to accept "pine time" as a part of the game. Use the time to watch and learn. If you find yourself "riding the pine," try not to miss anything that is going on so that when you are back in the game, you will be better than ever! Never doubt that you are *"God's workmanship, created in Christ Jesus to do good works, which God prepared in advance for us to do."* Ephesians 2:10. God never makes mistakes, and you were not created only to ride the pine on God's team. Your time is coming. Get ready to enter the game and watch how God will use your time on the sidelines to prepare you for the greatest works of your life!

26

Winning Through an Imitation

My hero growing up was the great New York Yankee center fielder, Mickey Mantle. He was from Commerce, Oklahoma, and since I grew up in Oklahoma City, it was natural for me to love "The Mick." I would copy him in every way I could. I tried to become a switch hitter, because he could do it. I tried to run faster, because he could run like the wind. I would even try to get the number seven as my jersey number, because that was Mickey's number.

Dale Mitchell, my dad, played ten years in the Major Leagues, first with the Cleveland Indians and then the Brooklyn Dodgers. My dad was a hero because of his incredible success as a Major League player. He had a lifetime batting average of .312 over ten years, and in Oklahoma in the 40s and 50s, he was a legend. The baseball field at the University of Oklahoma is named in his honor. One day, he quietly said to me, "Son, don't pull for Mantle. Don't try to be like him. He has some big problems and isn't what he appears to be. I would rather you have a hero like Harmon Killebrew of the Twins." I did not know how to receive this information, but it was my dad talking, so I listened and took his advice. Thirty years later Mickey confessed publicly to problems with alcohol and lifestyle. I still liked him even up until the day he died, but I was able to understand better why my dad had given me the advice he did. As an adult, I have had the great privilege to become friends with Harmon Killebrew. My dad was right about him too. He is one of the best people you could ever have as a hero in more ways than one. He is a gentleman in every sense of the word and has a passion for charitable work, especially those organizations that help kids in need.

As I grew older, my heroes in life truly were my sister, my brother, my mom and dad, my wife, Gari, and my children, Andy and Ashley. My brother, Dale Jr., was my hero as a kid because he would let me tag along and was always excelling in sports. He took the time to show me what it took to be an athlete. In my eyes, he was bigger than life. My sister, Lana, is one of the most care-giving people you will ever meet. As one who has received her love over and over, I always see her as a hero.

My wife and kids will always be heroes to me, mostly because of their amazing faith and support of me and each other during the tough times we have had as a family. When I think of them, I think of the finest qualities you could think of in another person. Their love, humor, courage, faithfulness, and patience with me will always rest positively in my mind. When my mother died in 1976, twelve different people wrote to tell us that "Margaret was the best friend I have ever had." She had a way of treating people that made everyone love her and consider her their "best friend!" She was an example of how we should treat each other and will always be one of my heroes.

Each season, I challenge our players to carefully consider who they are looking up to as heroes. Our heroes are important because sometimes, without even intending to, we become like them.

The best hero we can choose and who will never disappoint us, is our Lord Jesus Christ. Ephesians 5:1 says that we should *"be imitators of God; therefore, as dearly loved children, and live a life full of love, just as Christ loved us and gave Himself up for us as a fragrant offering and sacrifice to God."*

When asked, "How do I begin to imitate Christ," I usually refer to the Philippians 2: 6-8 where it says, *"Christ being in very nature God, did not consider equality with God something to be grasped, but made himself nothing, taking the very nature of a servant, being made in human likeness, and being formed in appearance to be a man, he humbled himself, and became obedient to death, even death on a cross."*

So, most importantly and as the best place to begin, we should imitate the humility expressed by Jesus Christ! For confident, competitive, high profile, strong-willed and successful people, this sometimes is "hard to swallow, much less follow!" You're telling me to be humble after all I've accomplished and accumulated? Yes, that is the first step. Recognize that we have nothing that He has not provided for us, and humility hopefully will soon follow.

Secondly, to imitate Christ, the Bible says we must offer ourselves as living sacrifices. Romans 12: 1 says, *"Therefore, I urge you brothers in view of God's mercy, to offer your bodies as living sacrifices, holy and pleasing to God—this is your spiritual act of worship. Do not conform any longer to the pattern of this world, but be transformed by the renewing of your mind."*

So, it is simple. If you want to imitate Christ, just be humble for starters, and then offer your bodies as living sacrifices!

There are so many benefits to be gained by having Christ as your hero. For example, unlike other heroes, He never lets us down. Hebrews 13:8 says *"Jesus Christ is the same yesterday, today, and forever."* His love for us is perfect, His care for us is thorough and long suffering, and His example is pure. What else can we possibly be looking for in a hero?

Many of the professional athletes have started wearing the "What Would Jesus Do" (WWJD) bracelets. As much as I admire the display, the commitment to continually ask that question before thinking or acting in situations is obviously more important. But asking that question does help us focus on Christ and not on ourselves.

When you follow the example of Christ and make Him your hero, ultimately your life will lead others to see Christ in you, and that indeed will be an incredible feeling of success!

By imitating Christ, our very nature will be "transformed into His likeness," and our ultimate Hero will have influenced and changed us to be the best we can possibly be!

27

Technical Fouls

Technical fouls are becoming more and more frequent in the NBA. A technical foul is usually called when a player or a coach loses control of their emotions and uses inappropriate or offensive language towards an official. Many times game officials overlook the insults and personal attacks. When they have had enough, however, they will blow the whistle and call a technical foul, resulting in free throws for the opposing team. If a player or coach happens to get two technical fouls in a game, he is automatically ejected from the game and fined by the league.

My seats for the Denver Nuggets games are at courtside, and I am amazed at the terrible language used by a lot of players in the league. Some of the players are so rude that you wonder if they are completely out of control off of the court too.

James 1:26 states, *"Anyone who says he is a Christian but doesn't control his sharp tongue is just fooling himself, and his religion isn't worth much."* This warning is for all of us, not just professional basketball players. In James 3:5-12 the warnings about controlling our tongues continues when it says, *"Likewise the tongue is a small part of the body, but it makes great boasts. Consider what a great forest is set on fire by a small spark. The tongue also is a fire, a world of evil among the parts of the body. It corrupts the whole person, sets the whole course of his life on fire, and is itself set on fire by hell.*

All kinds of animals, birds, reptiles, and creatures of the sea are being tamed and have been tamed by man, but no man can tame the tongue. It is a restless evil, full of deadly poison.

With the tongue we praise our Lord and Father, and with it we curse men, who have been made in God's likeness. Out of the same mouth come praise and cursing. My brothers, this should not be. Can both fresh water and salt water flow from the same spring? My brothers, can a fig tree bear olives, or a grapevine bear figs? Neither can a salt spring produce fresh water."

The players have told me that one of their favorite chapels is the one in which I deal with the tongue. To illustrate my point, I slice an orange in half and hold it in my hand. I then squeeze the orange until all of the juice has run out and into a bowl. I ask the players to tell me what comes out when you squeeze an orange? The answer is obviously orange juice, but I am asking for more than that. Eventually I tell them the answer is, "Whatever is *inside* comes out when you *squeeze* the orange." The players immediately understand and embrace the illustration and the mental picture of squeezing the orange. It reminds them that when we are squeezed as people, what we are really like inside is what will come out of us!

It is fairly easy to be a good guy and treat people with kindness and respect when every "call" is going our way. But when we get squeezed, only then can we tell what we are really like by what comes out of us! Someone cuts us off in traffic, we lose it and they are going to hear it from us! The cable company is a day late to install its system in our house, so when they do show up, we read them the riot act! How do you react to others, whether they are right or wrong?

I am *not* advocating that we become doormats. As Christians, the love of Christ and proper responses in terms of attitude and language should be consistently and increasingly the ways we handle problem situations. Why? First of all, for the sake of our own health and well being. Secondly, for the witness we are to others as a Christian. 2 Corinthians 6:3 says, *"We try to live in such a way that no one will ever be offended or kept back from finding the Lord by the way we act."*

People are watching and listening to you. Your example of how you are conducting yourself is of critical importance. To represent Christ is the highest honor an individual can have. We need to control ourselves and our tongues in an effort to represent Him in a way that brings honor and not disgrace to Him.

Ask yourself this question—If an NBA official followed me for a day, how many technical fouls would I receive? Would he throw me out of the game?

I actually look forward to getting "squeezed" so I can check on how I am doing inside! As I do, prepare in advance for your next squeezing by allowing the Holy Spirit to fill you and flow from you at all times. It honors the Lord, and it blesses people. It will make you feel clean, free, and better about yourself in the process!

Do not be discouraged if this has been a problem area for you. Be encouraged because you now understand that it is common to most people, and now you can set your mind on overcoming the problem! Look for an opportunity *today* to respond as God's man or woman, and you'll feel positive power that results from a proper, God-like reaction!

28

Playing to the Crowd

"Show Time" was the name given to the style of play that the L.A. Lakers brought to the NBA under the leadership of coach, Pat Riley. It was a fast paced style of action that excited the fans like never before. The style also helped the Lakers win a series of championships. They had great talent, coaching, character, and chemistry. They also began playing their games before the biggest crowds the game of basketball had ever seen. The Great Western Forum in the days of, "Show Time" became the place to be. The top Hollywood stars joined in the action and the Laker players rose to the occasion time and time again. Of course, they were doing their best for themselves, each other, their coaches, families and friends. But suddenly they realized that their audience was even greater than they had imagined, and they seemed to play best to that huge audience who shared in the thrills of "Show Time."

As popular and effective as "Show Time" was, playing to the crowd has also been the downfall of many NBA players and many people in life. Often a player will try too many fancy moves with the basketball just to entertain the crowds. Maybe it is a behind the back pass, or an acrobatic hammer dunk. Whatever the case, it becomes obvious to his teammates and coaches that he has an orientation toward something other than winning as a team.

As Christian men and women, we are to have a Christ orientation. By this I mean that we should live to please Christ with what we say and do, or do not say and do not do. Our thinking and our actions that follow should be motivated only by focusing on the question, would Christ approve of what I am doing? We have all been an offender of this teaching. For years I personally lived in confusion and caused myself, my family, and my friends a great deal of suffering because I had a *project* and a *people* orientation. My "audiences" literally had become other people and the projects I was working on at the time. I was driven by this orientation and not by Christ and His Lordship in my life. It was unintentional but very damaging.

The Bible is clear that when we claim to be Christians, we are to *"Be careful how we act: these are difficult days. Don't be fools; be wise and make the most of every opportunity you have for doing good. Don't act thoughtlessly, but try to find out and do whatever the Lord wants you to."* (Living Bible, Ephesians 5:15-17) Another pertinent verse is, Colossians 3:23, *"Whatever you do, work at it with all your heart, as working for the Lord, not for men."*

That sounds so simple doesn't it? How should we live? Well, "find out and do whatever the Lord wants you to!" A Christ orientation would protect us in our actions and our speech because we would always seek to find out first what the Lord would have us to do and say.

In the past my people orientation got me in trouble over and over again. Without realizing it, I had become a puppet! I lived for the approval of man and eventually almost destroyed my witness and my life because of it. I also was continuously using poor leadership skills with people because I had a project orientation. If God gave me a task to complete, that is what drove me. I unintentionally hurt many people along the way but eventually learned that God's people and my love for them was much more important than any project!

1 Peter 1:14 says, *"Obey God because you are his children: don't slip back into your old ways—doing evil because you knew no better. Be holy in everything you do, just as the Lord is holy, who invited you to be his child."* To fully obey God, a Christ orientation is a must. Playing to any other audience will cause us to drift away from Him and into self-destructive nonsense.

Some people are oriented to pleasure. Others have a money orientation and spend their lives in the pursuit of the almighty dollar. The list is long, but I think you get the idea. Ask yourself in the same way I ask our ballplayers, what is my orientation? Who is my audience? Then, read 1 Peter 1:3 that says, *"All honor to God, the God and Father of our Lord Jesus Christ: for it is His boundless mercy that has given us the privilege of being born again, so that we are now members of God's own family."*

As you ponder this verse, consider the joy that can be yours if you play out the days of your life for an audience of One!

29

Decision Making

Basketball is much like the game of life in terms of the number of decisions that have to be made quickly and decisively in order to come out ahead. Both are very fast paced and require an ability to think on the move. In basketball, there is even a shot clock which limits each offensive possession of a team to only 24 seconds. If the team with the ball fails to get a shot off within the 24 seconds, the ball goes to the other team. There is no time to waste; decisions must be made quickly!

As in basketball, there are some key elements to consider when making decisions as Christians. Most people want to make the right choices for themselves and their families, but sometimes do not have the "tools" in place to do so and suffer the consequences of a bad choice.

A tool that helps me to make good decisions was given to me by my spiritual mentor while I was in college. Dan Stavely was on the football coaching staff at University of Colorado and led our Fellowship of Christian Athletes' groups. FCA. was open to everyone, so even though I played baseball and basketball, Coach Stavely still became like a second father to me. For example, he was the first person I called when Gari and I got engaged. After I told him, he said, "That's great, Bo, but it's 2:00 a.m., are you sure this couldn't have waited until the morning?" He is smart, funny, and a very close friend.

I went to him one evening struggling in a couple of areas

as a new Christian. His wisdom and advice were a great help to me as evidenced by the fact that 32 years later I am sharing with the Denver Nuggets at chapel what he taught me so long ago. This is the tool he gave me when he instructed me never to make an important decision until I had asked myself the following four questions:

What does the Bible say about this decision, if anything?

What do wise, Christian counselors who love me and want the best for me think I should do?

What do the circumstances tell me is the correct decision to make?

What does my "inner voice" reveal to me after I have prayed about this?

He told me that I should think about all four questions every time I made an important decision. He advised me to use the questions almost as a grid through which I should see and filter every important decision. I have never forgotten his lesson, and his wisdom has helped me many times. The players I have shared this with through the years find this to be a valuable tool. They have told me that the simplicity of this tool allows them to quickly use it when they need it the most.

The other key concept Coach Stavely taught me in regards to decision making was to, "Never make a major decision during a down time." Give yourself time to recover and refill your tank before you tackle a difficult decision. This has helped me to avoid unnecessary quick responses or decisions when a little time would have helped me think better. In other words, take more time when decisions have long reaching effects and spend less time when they do not.

Years after the Coach helped me, I was privileged to hear Henry Blackaby speak on the subject of decision making. I had completed Blackaby's study guide entitled, *Experiencing God,* and I liked the man and his style long before I had the privilege of meeting him or hearing him speak. I knew when I first heard his thoughts on decision making, this material had to be shared with my small congregation of NBA players. I took careful notes during his sermon and chose these factors of decision making as important lessons to learn. Each year now, Blackaby's message on decision making becomes part of one of our team's chapel services. They are as follows:

Factors of Decision Making

Make decisions preeminently by faith – (Heb. 11:6)

> Ask yourself – is this decision based on absolute trust in God?

Make decisions based on your relationship to Christ – (John 14:21, 23)

> God has the right to give you directives.

Make decisions based on Scripture

> Always seek a clear word from God from His Word.

Make decisions based on Prayer

> Talk to the Lord, listen, and stay there until He speaks.

Make decisions based on the council of wise Christians that God has given you – (Prov. 11:14)

> There is "safety" in seeking council.

Make decisions out of obedience to God not convenience

> It is not your comfort that is the critical element.

Make decisions remembering that you are accountable to God – (2 Cor. 5:9)

> The farther you go with God, the more you realize what He can do.

Make decisions asking yourself the question, "What would Jesus do?"

> He is seeking to live out His life in you – (Gal. 2:20).

You are on the "court" of life, and the better you become at making good decisions, the better you will play the "game" of life!

30

Road Trip of Life

A great comedian has a routine he does about "stuff." He talks about how people collect so much stuff they have to buy houses just to store all of their stuff. He points out that people naturally compare their stuff to other people's stuff, even going so far as to say, "My stuff is good stuff, and your stuff is not so good!" At some point in his show, he says problems occur when people go on vacation. They must decide what stuff to pack and take with them on the road and what stuff to leave behind! The vacation part of the presentation caused me to think about the stuff I pack, not only for trips, but especially for my "road trip of life."

As this comedian said, we all tend to clutter our lives with the stuff of the world. We sometimes buy things we do not really need. We make commitments with our time that take us away from what is truly important. Plus, we end up with questions like, "Why did I do that or buy that?"

NBA players make a lot of money. They are at an age when "stuff" has great appeal. I try to teach our guys that God is the giver of every good and perfect gift in life. (James 1:17) Problems occur when we get things out of balance and we fill the spaces in our lives with the "stuff" of the world, instead of the gifts God has intended for us.

One night at chapel just before our team was to leave on a four game, ten day road trip, I focused on this concept of "packing only what you need to serve God" for this long and wonderful "road trip" we call life. Experienced travelers learn how much baggage is just the right amount. They take only what they need and leave behind the nonessentials that would be a burden. To be effective and move about more unrestricted and free, they make the choice to travel light.

The Bible is clear about the fact that we are only on this earth for a short time before we join Jesus in heaven. (James 4:14) We are only passing through and must concentrate on not becoming ensnared by the trappings of burdensome baggage and stuff that the world has to offer. 2 Timothy 2:4 says, *"No soldier in active service entangles himself in the affairs of everyday life, so that he may please the one who enlisted him as a soldier."*

How we go through this life depends a lot on what each of us decides is essential in the things we own, the attachments we form, the time commitments we make, and the truths we allow to shape our lives.

It becomes necessary to prepare in advance for this journey, just like the players think through what to pack for a long NBA road trip. We should want only what we need, because we are on the move. If we are truly about God's business and the things of His Kingdom, it may require that we rid ourselves of some "stuff" that continues to slow us down or get in our way.

At the conclusion of this chapel service, I ask our guys to consider some of these questions, and I ask you to do the same:

What possessions do I have that cause more trouble and
   worry than they are worth?
Do I weigh myself down by longing for more than I really
   need, to be God's man or woman?
Have I unintentionally fallen into a flirtation with worldly

things that have taken me away from God?

Do I waste God's valuable time and energy on things that do not really matter?

Does the desire for bigger, better, and more crowd out the desire to know Jesus more?

If I were told today that I had only one year to live, what would I let go of and what would I hold on to?

God wants to use us as His mouth, feet, hands, and ears. We are His representatives, and we should have God in mind when we consider what we need or do not need while traveling on this "road trip of life." It can be a journey full of peace, joy, balance, love, and all of God's blessings, or it can be a journey full of distractions, pain, confusion, loneliness, and suffering. The choice in many cases is ours, and the "stuff" we pack for the trip will contribute to how encumbered or unencumbered we are as we travel as His representative going about His business!

In other words, what you pack or do not pack greatly determines your joy as you travel your "road trip of life." Throw out the excess baggage that is keeping you from being all God intended you to be!

31

Integrity

In the off season, I occasionally get the chance to play golf with some of the Denver Nuggets. It is always enjoyable to see them away from the pressures of the season. They are fierce competitors, even at golf, so the game is on when we tee it up!

Two of the team's players and a friend of mine named Howard Parker had just hit our drives on the second hole one afternoon when we were approached by one of the assistant pros at the course. He said to us, "Were any of you hitting your drivers off of the practice tee today? A boy was hit in the head and has been taken to the hospital." He went on to explain that drivers were not allowed that day on the range because the tees were so far forward that the range was too short to contain long drives. What happened next was very revealing to me about my friends, and myself. I was the first one to speak up and I said, "Since I'm the member here, I'm sure I'm the one who hit the kid. Let me take care of this and you guys keep playing." Then, one of our star players said, "No, the fact is I have a large insurance policy for situations just like this and I'm sure I'm the one who hit him." Finally, the second ball player in our group said, " The fact is, I'm probably the one who hit him because I remember seeing two or three shots go over that hill! Please, let me take care of it!"

Very quickly we all agreed that our golf was over for that day. The players wanted to go to the hospital to check on the young boy and his family. Not trying to be a jerk, but simply to give perspective, I said, "Are you guys sure you want to personally have contact with this family, because once they see who you are it could cause problems?"

My friends were even stronger than I thought they were because nothing mattered to them except getting to the hospital and checking on that boy. It was the right thing to do. They acted without hesitation, and I saw integrity in action that day. Oh, by the way, the ball had hit the ground first, and by the time it bounced up and hit the boy, it did not have much power left, so it didn't really injure him. The trip to the hospital was mostly precautionary, but he was very excited to meet these men of integrity who also happened to be Denver Nuggets players!

Absolute integrity is a necessary ingredient that is missing so often in peoples' lives. We have learned to fudge the truth or exaggerate the circumstances. I have done it and regret it and pray I am over the habit. The full story, the complete truth, the dedication to follow through on a promise all constitute ingredients of integrity.

When I speak to the players at chapel, I begin by giving them the definition of integrity. Integrity is an "unimpaired condition of soundness and the quality of being complete or undivided." As Christians, it is a conviction of the spirit and of emotion. Integrity is not something that is arrived at logically, and it always goes hand in hand with the Bible.

Integrity consists of:
Stability
Consistency
Openness
Follow through
Integrity is not:

Dishonesty
Deception
Half-truths
Honesty
Unjust treatment of others

Integrity can be the backbone of an individual or team, or when it is lacking a back breaker of both. In terms of our commitment to family, friends, or team, I believe integrity is defined as, "Saying what you promise to do, and then doing your best to follow it through to completion!"

Many of the broken lives we see all around us today are directly related to the lack of integrity. People just do not follow through on their stated or implied promises. I have been on both sides of this problem and regret the times I have failed and then been disappointed when others have failed me. I thank God that He is in the business of fresh starts, second chances, and new beginnings! I am thankful that as we grow in our relationship with Christ, He reveals to us, through scripture and prayer, the deeper meaning of the word integrity.

If you are looking for an example of absolute integrity, look no further than Jesus. There was never a rushed pace or a hurried moment. There was never an unattractive encounter because *truth* has a way of cutting through nonsense.

People were and are drawn to Him, and they will be drawn to you if you choose to walk in His shoes and exercise absolute integrity in everything you do and say.

Most importantly, the cornerstone of *character* is integrity. In other words, if you cannot trust people at one point in his or her life, it is very difficult to trust them at *any* point in their lives. So, draw a new line in the sand and decide for yourself to exercise integrity in every area of your life, so that you can have the character that is pleasing to God.

32

Forgiveness

For ten years I had a very close friend called "Doc." I met him when he was 89 years old, and he in many ways was like my father until the day he died just 40 days short of his 100th birthday. I loved spending time with Doc because he never lost his zeal for living and learning. We would go to lunch together, talk on the phone for what seemed to be forever, or just sit around in his apartment visiting and drinking iced tea.

Often times, I would play a modified version of word association with Doc. As soon as I would launch into the routine, he would pick right up on it and off we would go. I would simply ask him a series of rapid-fire questions about all sorts of subjects and he would respond with a one-word answer or quick phrase.

The most memorable response for me was when I asked him what had been the key to his long and happy marriage. He quickly said, "Forgiveness." On this one, my follow up question was, "Why that word?" His answer was great! He said "Marriage is a lot of time together, and lots of things happen so you must be quick to forgive!"

At the time, I had only been married for a few years, so I did not fully understand the wisdom in Doc's advice. Now, 30 years into my married life with my wife, Gari, I am thankful for his wisdom and credit him with teaching me one of life's great lessons. Forgiveness is a lesson that is needed for every relationship, not just marriage.

Basketball at the NBA level is so fast paced and fiercely competitive that tempers flare almost every game. There are fights with opponents and even arguments with teammates and coaches. I try to ask the players who choose to come to chapel to become ambassadors of peace. I instruct them in the Biblical truth regarding forgiveness. It is an art that should be learned and practiced by all Christians. The rewards of being a forgiving person are peace, happiness, freedom, and joy, among many others. The consequences of being an unforgiving person are harmful. Your anger turns inward and you become guilty, or you slowly grow bitter, never better. You get more prideful and stubborn because you will not give in and ask for nor grant forgiveness. Ultimately, you choose your own medicine with God in terms of His forgiveness towards you because the Bible says in Matthew 6:14-15, *"For if you forgive men when they sin against you, your heavenly Father will also forgive you. But if you do not forgive men their sins, your father will not forgive your sins."*

You call your own shots in terms of how you will be dealt with by your actions towards others! Here is another very important message in Matthew 5:21-25. *"You have heard that it was said to the people long ago, 'Do not murder, and anyone who murders will be subject to judgment.' But I tell you that anyone who is angry with his brother will be subject to judgment. Again, anyone who says to his brother, 'Raca,' is answerable to the Sanhedrin. But anyone who says, 'You fool!' will be in danger of the fire of hell."*

"Therefore, if you are offering your gift at the altar and there remember that your brother has something against you, leave your gift there in front of the altar. First go and be reconciled to your brother; then come and offer your gift."

"Settle matters quickly with your adversary who is taking you to

*court. Do it while you are still with him on the way, or he may hand
you over to the judge, and the judge may hand you over to the officer, and you may be thrown into prison."*

These verses say that God is not interested in a sacrifice
from you if you have not done your part in seeking reconciliation with someone who has something against you. No matter
if it is us or the other person who is at fault, we are called to be
the peacemakers.

I try to workout everyday to stay healthy and in shape. The
most difficult part of my workout is usually the *first step*. I find
it is that way with forgiveness too. We let grudges and hard
feelings grow and grow because we are not willing to take the
first step. Ephesians 4:31-32 says, *"Get rid of all bitterness, rage,
and anger, brawling and slander, along with every form of malice.
Be kind and compassionate to one another, forgiving each other, just
as Christ forgave you."*

This type of forgiveness requires work on our part. When
someone is offended and we are the cause, we should take
responsibility to clear the slate and seek forgiveness. If we are
the one who has been offended, we can still take the first step
by saying, "Can we get together and work this thing through?"

It is a shame when problems occur and the only solution
that people can think of is to destroy the relationship completely and part company on bad terms. It might be the very
reason for so much divorce these days. Many are not interested in working at forgiveness.

I know there are examples where one party is not going to
be honest about their contribution to the conflict. When this
occurs, our responsibility to them and God is to continue to do
our best to bring about reconciliation. God is in the miracle
business and there may be no greater miracle than the loving

forgiveness He extends to us. The least we should do is to make an effort to extend that same love and forgiveness to each other.

If there is someone you need to call or visit to initiate the forgiveness process, I encourage you not to hesitate for another moment. You will be glad that you took the responsibility to do your part because God will bless you for becoming a peacemaker!

33

The Value of Humor

Richard Beach is the founder and president of Doulos Ministries in Denver, Colorado. For over 20 years, Doulos has trained Christian leaders, helped troubled teens, and operated inner city camps that have witnessed thousands of conversions to Christ. He is one of the best friends I have ever had and a dynamic leader. Of all of his leadership abilities, it is his sense of humor that I enjoy the most. He is able to laugh at himself and put people at ease while doing so. He is a combination of Jay Leno (who is funny) and Billy Graham (who is spiritual). If you spend time with him, you will both laugh and cry! For example, on one occasion a man handed Rich a donation to Doulos for $10,000. With great emotion, the man said, "Rich, I can't tell you how much you and your ministry have helped my family and me." Rich gently placed his hand on the man's shoulder, and with a twinkle in his eye looked at him and said, "You should have seen what I'd have done to help you and your family for $20,000!" The man and Rich are close friends or Rich would not have said what he said. I tell this story because it illustrates why I find him such fun to be with. By the way, a month later the man sent another $10,000 donation!

I have invited Richard a number of times to speak at a Nuggets pre-game chapel service. The Nuggets organization has asked me to minimize the number of guest speakers I bring to chapel because of privacy issues for the players. I agree with their philosophy and follow their instruction. But on occasion, I will ask Rich to share with the guys.

There are a number of reasons for feeling good about Rich coming. His messages are great, and he knows how to handle himself in this sports atmosphere. But the primary reason I ask him to speak to the players is because of his sense of humor. He has a personal magnetism that draws the players to him and makes them feel comfortable. He has had plenty of suffering in his life, but he has always dealt with it by saying, "Affliction colors your life, but you get to choose the color!" He is not shallow in terms of how he thinks and deals with people. Instead, he is very tuned in to the players needs and looks for the tasteful time to lift their spirits with a touch of humor. Some of my most memorable belly laughs at chapel have been with him, and I continually want our players to experience that, too.

Usually after encountering Rich at chapel, I will spend a service on the subject of humor with our players. I will use Rich as an example of how humor can play a role in healing our spirits. As an illustration, I will try to get the players to ease each other's burdens by getting them to share something funny in their lives as a way to loosen things up. Too often, the burden of life draws us into a downward spiral that we find difficult to escape. I try to provide just a moment of escape from the players' pressure packed lives by helping them understand that humor is from God! He is the one who gives us that ability to laugh and see the humor and fun in life. That is why humor should never be nasty, sarcastic, or hurtful. God means it to lift us, not hurt us. I have misused humor in my life and still have to concentrate on using it appropriately.

There is no place which should be as comfortable for NBA

players as their home locker room. It turns into a difficult place to be if one or two bad apples have spoiled the climate with their negativity or self-centeredness. On the other hand, put a good-natured jokester or two in their midst and that locker room turns into a place of comfort, joy, peace, and acceptance.

This past season, our guys were "welcoming" a rookie to the team, using humor as a way to help him feel accepted. On one road trip, they told the rookie that the pair of shoes he had on were "not attractive—and he should never wear them again or there would be a price to pay." The shoes were expensive, and I kind of liked them. They were a tan suede with brown leather heels and soles. Well, the rookie wore the shoes to a home game a few weeks later, and while he was out doing some early shooting with one of the coaches, his teammates took the shoes from his locker and every player autographed them with a big, black Sharpie pen! They had a blast doing it, and the rookie got a good laugh, too.

From my perspective, the team appeared to be closer than ever that night as they laughed together. Ecclesiastes 3:4 says that there is *"A time to weep and a time to laugh."* I am certain that Jesus and his disciples spent hours laughing together. It is good medicine for all kinds of sickness, and I pray that if you have a sense of humor, you will use it properly to lift up those around you! If you do not have a sense of humor, take the necessary steps to contribute with the gifts God has given you, but learn to laugh along the way!

34

Teamwork

The author of this piece is unknown, but from the first time I read it, I knew it was one of the best description of the need for teamwork I have ever read. This is the story of a bricklayer who had tried to move about five hundred pounds of bricks from the top of a four-story building to the sidewalk below. The problem was, he tried to do it alone. In his own words (taken from his insurance claim form)…

"It would have taken too long to carry the bricks down by hand, so I decided to put them in a barrel and lower them by a pulley which I had fastened to the top of the building. After tying the rope securely at the ground level, I then went up to the top of the building. I fastened the rope around the barrel, loaded it with the bricks and swung it out over the sidewalk for the descent. Then I went down to the sidewalk and untied the rope, holding it securely to guide the barrel down slowly. But, since I weigh only one hundred forty pounds, the five hundred pound load jerked me from the ground so fast that I didn't have time to think of letting go of the rope. And as I passed between the second and third floors, I met the barrel coming down. This accounts for the bruises and lacerations on my upper body. I held tightly to the rope until I reached the top, where my hand became jammed in the pulley. This accounts for my broken thumb. At the same time, however, the barrel hit the sidewalk with a bang and the bottom fell out. With the weight of the bricks gone, the barrel

weighed only about forty pounds. Thus my one hundred forty pound body began a swift descent, and I met the empty barrel coming up. This accounts for my sprained back and broken collarbone. At this point, I lost my presence of mind completely and let go of the rope, and the empty barrel came crashing down on me. This accounts for my head injuries. As for the last question on the form—what would you do if the same situation arose again? – Please be advised that I am finished trying to do the job alone."

This guy needed a team!

The great NBA teams always seem to have super stars. The Lakers had Magic Johnson, the Celtics had Larry Bird, and the Bulls had Michael Jordan. Eventually, all these teams won one or more NBA championships. But, the championship rings came only after the stars understood that in order to win they had to play within the structure of the team. One man could not do it alone. In fact, if any one player tried to, it caused all kinds of problems and produced an average team.

As Christians, we are part of the team which is the Body of Christ. First Corinthians 12:12-20 describes our team when it says, *"The body is a unit, though it is made up of many parts: and though all its parts are many, they form one body. So it is with Christ. For we were all baptized by one Spirit into one body— whether Jew or Greek, slave or free—and we were all given the one Spirit to drink. Now the body is not made up of one part, but of many. If the foot should say, "Because I am not a hand, I do not belong to the body, it would not for that reason cease to be part of the body. And if the ear should say, 'Because I am not an eye, I do not belong to the body,' it would not for that reason cease to be part of the body. If the whole body were an eye, where would the sense of hearing be? If the whole body were an ear, where would the sense of smell be? But in fact God has arranged the parts of the body, every one of them, just as he wanted them to be. If they were all one part, where would the body be? As it is, there are many parts, but one body." Verse 27 says, "Now you are the body of Christ, and each one of you is a part of it."*

In the sport of basketball, there must be players who can rebound, shoot, pass, dribble, play defense, and run the court. Once in a while, coaches find a player who can "do it all," but this is rare. So when they form a team they look for gifted guys to excel in specific spots. The key is getting the right team together, so the players can function in the areas of their strength.

As Christians, the same is true. We must first understand who we are, our function on Christ's team. Then we must understand and accept the concept of dying to "self" in order to serve the Body of Christ. When we do not need to defend ourselves, we have died to ourselves. When we are content with our status in life and do not demand "bigger, better, and more" at every turn, we have died to ourselves. When we can receive correction and reproof without rebellion or resentment, we have died to ourselves.

When you love to give God the glory and not refer to yourself for the credit of a success, you are on your way to dying to yourself. It is not about you. It is about Him and His team, the Body of Christ.

As teammates, we should lift up our Coach first and foremost—Jesus Christ our Lord and Savior. Then lift up each other as we strive to be all that we are capable of being on the greatest Team ever assembled!

35

Role Players

Some of my favorite people who have played for the Denver Nuggets over the past eight seasons have been guys that are called "role players." These players are not usually the starters or the stars of the team. These are the guys who are asked to come off the bench for ten to twenty-five minutes a game and perform a specific task. Some guys are asked to give the team an offensive surge by scoring points quickly. Others are asked to play a pounding, physical game for the purpose of intimidating the opponent. Still others may be asked to pick up the slack in rebounding. What I have noticed is that these players, the ones that know and embrace their role, seem to be the happiest, most content players in the NBA. They still have the pressure of preparing and performing, but knowing <u>exactly</u> what is expected of them seems to "free them up" to enjoy and celebrate their role on the team.

The players who are not sure of their roles are quite the opposite. They are almost like the old story of the rabbit on the swim team. Obviously, rabbits would be better off on the track team instead where they can excel in their natural talent. In the same way, players can get very frustrated when their talents are not being fully used. The coaches get frustrated too and lose perspective on a player's talent when they are not in the right spot. The result is that everybody suffers, and no one wins.

I have encouraged our players through the years to take

the time to learn what their spiritual gifts are in order to play the key role God has for them on His team. The Bible is clear about these gifts, yet Christians do not study them enough to discover what God designed them to be and do.

The apostle Paul shares a list of the spiritual gifts in three different chapters in three separate epistles. They are as follows:

Romans 12:3-8 1	1 Cor. 12:8-10 28-30	Eph. 4:11
Prophecy	Word of Wisdom	Apostleship
Ministering	Word of Knowledge	Prophesy
Teaching	Faith	Evangelism
Exhorting	Healing	Pastoring
Giving	Miracles	Teaching
Government	Prophecy	
Showing mercy	Discernment	
	Tongues	
	Interpretation	
	Apostleship	
	Teaching	
	Administration	
	Government	

Not every spiritual gift is listed in these columns, yet most can be found here. It is important to point out that these gifts are not the same as human talents. Even non-believers possess talents like painting, speaking, playing basketball, and many others. However; these are only talents, not spiritual gifts. Only believers have gifts like those listed above. Talents can benefit everyone but only on a natural level. Spiritual gifts relate to supernatural happenings and power in the life of the one who is exercising the gift.

The gifts listed do not indicate godliness in our life. You do not *earn* the gifts by building your spiritual muscle to a certain point. The gifts are *given* by God when we accept Christ as our Savior. Gifts must be used and exercised to grow spiritually. We become better at serving the body of Christ as we grow in an understanding of our spiritual gifting and keep using those gifts over a consistent period of time.

When I think of myself at age 30, as compared to where I am now at age 50, some things make me both anxious and sad. Anxious because of how many times I should have done that which I did not do, and sad because of the wonderful people I hurt along the way by improperly exercising a gift from God that should have been used more wisely. I did not blow it all the time, but enough times that I have regrets. My *position* with the gifts was great: As God had given certain gifts to me to be used for Him. My *condition* as His man was too immature and I used the gifts in a wrong way.

As the Nuggets players are much better at performing to their full abilities when their specific role on the team is clearly defined we are better as Christians when we have taken the time to *discover*, then *develop* our spiritual gifts so that we can function and live out our best to the glory of God.

If this is an area you have never spent much time researching, I encourage you to do so. No matter how well developed and blessed you are in the area of human talents, you will never be complete until you identify and begin functioning in the area of *your* spiritual gifts.

36

Twelve Tips So Men Can Win

Each season, I do two chapels on quick hitting "tips" for the Nuggets ball players. These tips are designed to be simple, to the point, with a scripture that teaches the lesson better than any man today could. The players seem to latch on to one or two of the 12 tips, depending on what they are going through at that time in their life. I wrote these tips at the conclusion of a difficult time in my life. I was creating a tool that would help me to overcome, and not merely survive my difficulties. I hope one or more of these help you, too!

1. **Don't Take too long – to admit when you are wrong!**
   1 John 1:8 "If we claim to be without sin, we deceive ourselves and the truth is not in us."
   Be quick to say, "I am sorry—I was wrong."

2. **Identify, confess, and forget your sins – He died on the cross so you could win!**
   1 John 1:9-10 "If we confess our sins, He is faithful and just and will forgive us our sins and purify us from all unrighteousness. If we claim to be without sin, we make him out to be a liar, and His work has no place in our lives."
   God wants to give us new starts and fresh beginnings!

3.   **You can overcome anything, if your faith is in the King.**
     John 3:3 "I tell you the truth, no one can see the king-
     dom of God unless he is born again."
     2 Corinthians 5:17 "Therefore, if anyone is in Christ, he
     is a new creation...the old has gone, the new has
     come!"
     Faith in anything but God is not wise!

4.   **To avoid a mental riot, get alone with God and be quiet!**
     Phil. 4:6-7 "Do not be anxious about anything, but in
     everything by prayer and petition, with thanksgiving,
     present your requests to God, and the peace of God,
     which transcends all understanding, will guard your
     hearts and your minds in Christ Jesus."
     Don't have too much action and fast paced living!

5.   **Read your Bible everyday or there may be hell to pay!**
     Hebrews 4:12 "For the Word of God is living and
     active, sharper than any double-edged sword, it pene-
     trates, even to dividing soul and spirit, joint and mar-
     row, it judges the thoughts and attitudes of the heart."
     **The answers we need are in God's Love Letter to
     us—His Holy Scripture!**

6.   **Every single day—take the time to pray**
     1 Thessalonians 5:16-18 "Be joyful always, pray con-
     tinually, give thanks in all circumstances for this is
     God's will for you in Christ Jesus."
     **Communication with God is key to a healthy rela-
     tionship.**

7.   **To set your heart and mind on things above, concentrate
     on building your ladder of love. (Chapter 19)**

Colossians 3:1-2 "Since, then, you have been raised with Christ, set your hearts on things above, where Christ is seated at the right hand of God. *Set* your *minds* on things above, not on earthly things."

Matthew 22:37-39 Jesus replied: "Love the Lord your God with all your heart and with all your soul and with all your mind. This is the first and greatest commandment. And the second is like it: Love your neighbor as yourself."

Focus on relationships!

8. **Honor your wife—everyday of your life!**

    Ephesians 5:25 "Each one of you must love his wife, as he loves himself."

    You'll only have one life partner—love her, honor her, cherish her!

9. **The Law of the Harvest you must know—you'll eventually reap the seeds that you sow.**

    Galatians 6:7-8 "Do not be deceived, God cannot be mocked. A man reaps what he sows. The one who sows to reap his sinful nature, from that nature will reap destruction. The one who sows to please the Spirit, from the Spirit will reap eternal life."

    Plant, plant, and keep on planting!

10. **Take daily action to communicate – write, call, encourage—love in action is great!**

    James 2:17 "In the same way, Faith, by itself, if not accompanied by action, is dead."

    Be the one responsible for staying in touch!

11. **Do not get entangled in worldly affairs; keeping things simple will limit your cares.**

    2 Timothy 2:4 "No soldier in active service entangles himself in the affairs of everyday life, so that he may please the one who enlisted him as the soldier."

    Simple is better!

12. **No matter how deep you are in the hole—remember that God is still in control.**

    Revelation 4:2 "At once I was in the spirit, and there before me was a throne in Heaven with someone sitting on it!"

    You're a student in God's school; learn and move on to the next lesson.

Sometimes it is the quick reminders that help us to reform our thinking. The idea behind the "tips" is to help us get unstuck. Are you feeling "out of sorts" today? Maybe one of these tips will help you to get back on track and live victoriously!

37

Anxiety

Life is like an NBA game in so many ways. Anxious moments will most certainly occur in both. Because of that fact, I consider it a given that at some point during the NBA season I am going to commit one chapel service to the topic, "How do you handle anxiety?"

Philippians 4:5-11 is a great place to begin. It says, *"Let your gentleness be evident to all. The Lord is near. Do not be anxious about anything, but in everything, by prayer and petition, with thanksgiving, present your requests to God. And the peace of God, which transcends all understanding, will guard your hearts and your minds in Christ Jesus.*

Finally, brothers, whatever is true, whatever is noble, whatever is right, whatever is pure, whatever is lovely, whatever is admirable – if anything is excellent or praiseworthy – think about such things. Whatever you have learned or received or heard from me, or seen in me – put it into practice. And the God of peace will be with you.

I rejoice greatly in the Lord that at last you have renewed your concern for me. Indeed, you have been concerned, but you had no opportunity to show it. I am not saying this because I am in need, for I have learned to be content whatever the circumstances."

There are many principles that Paul teaches in this passage that we need to consider. But most importantly, I encourage our players to think about the passage *"do not be anxious about anything."* Setting their minds on this principle frees them to concentrate on playing the game and not on any impending doom that could occur—like missing a shot or losing the game. The ability to recognize an anxiety but control your mind to "think about things that are true, noble, right, pure and lovely" can be an incredible benefit. Be it basketball or life, the idea here is that it is human nature to feel anxious, but it should be a Christian's nature to handle it in such a way as to not paralyze or even hinder our "performance."

Picture yourself playing defense for Denver and the score is tied and Michael Jordan of the Bulls is the man you are assigned to guard. As he dribbles the ball slowly towards you, you want to be playing your best and concentrating on the task at hand, not preoccupied with the anxiety of the confrontation! In this example, adding the extra hardship of anxiety would almost certainly guarantee defeat.

Christians are to live free of this burden. Anxiety can divide your mind and pull you in directions that you do not need to be pulled. It distracts you from whatever it is you are trying to do and leaves you confounded. Anxiety also drains you of energy. In an NBA game, just like in life, negative energy is damaging to an individual's ability to play or live life to the "max." There are certain situations that present themselves to us that require all that we have, and we cannot afford to be drained at those critical moments! In life, when anxiety steals our peace and joy, it truly is a tragedy. Think about a person you know who is almost literally paralyzed by anxiety rather than living in the joy of Jesus.

It is not where God wants us to be. He wants us in a constant state of prayer—"pray without ceasing"—to guard our minds against the damage that anxiety can cause. Are there things that we should be concerned about or need our attention? Sure! Are there people and situations that may cause harm to us or bring difficulties into our lives? Of course! Does God want us weak, frantic, and pre-occupied due to anxiety as we think about or face those people or things? No! In fact he wants us to get our heads screwed on right by having a *God-view* of things. He is in control, He loves us, He prepares us for whatever it is we are going to face, and He expects us to *think* and *act* like adult Christians—not scared kids!

Our thoughts lead to the actions we take. If we are looking for the right and proper actions in life that lead to victories and successful living, it only makes sense that we first must *think* right. Fear and anxiety should become our enemies. I ask my players, what do you see when you look in the eyes of the greatest NBA players during crunch time? They typically say, "There is a calm confidence about them!"

As Christians who are sold out to a God that is completely in control of our lives should we not have even a larger dose of this calm confidence? Should it not be obvious to everyone who comes in contact with us?

Whatever the world wants to throw at you will not upset or even alter God's plan for your life. He loves you. He is in control, and He expects you to act on your faith in Him and do your best—nothing more is required. However, your best starts between your ears with how you think! Let His love and His grace and your confidence in Him occupy your mind and not anxiety. Overcome (not just merely survive) those moments in your life when anxiety poses a threat to your mental and emotional poise! Set your mind on Christ, and He will give you His peace which transcends all understanding!

38

Losing a Loved One

Losing a game is one thing. Losing a loved one is an entirely different story.

At the close of chapel each night, I ask the guys if they have any special prayer requests for me to include in my closing prayer. Usually the players say something like, "Pray for our injury situation" or "Please pray for my family back home."

One night, one of our star players who is a giant of a man, but with a childlike spirit and wonderful personality said, "Bo, please pray for me and my family. My uncle was murdered last night in New York City and it has been a tough time for us all." I looked at my friend for what seemed like forever before saying, "Come with me. We need to go let your coaches know about the pain you are feeling tonight—you owe that to them." He and I walked down the hall, and I left him alone with the head coach to discuss what had happened.

His news obviously put into perspective for all of us the ultimate insignificance of the game the Nuggets were about to play. Our thoughts were focused on our friend and his family. Our hearts were burdened and heavy with grief.

Have you ever received a call like my friend did? On January 5, 1987 at 8:00 a.m., my sister Lana, called me at my office in Denver to tell me, "Dad has suffered a heart attack this morning." My response was, "Is he okay?" to which she tenderly replied, "No, he didn't make it." Wow! What an alarming call! My dad had died!

You may have had a similar experience. If so, you know what it feels like to be totally caught off guard and have your breath literally taken away. Everyone goes through an experience like this at some point. After my friend told me about his uncle's murder, I thought it was appropriate for me to share with our players at our next chapel what a proper and healthy response to the loss of a loved one should be as a Christian.

First, I taught the players how only God knows the depths of our sorrow. I believe that the Bible teaches that God alone knows how bad a person is hurting. So, it is healthy and wise not to expect others to understand or be completely sensitive to how bad you may be feeling when you have lost someone: Unrealistic expectations of how friends should act towards you can cause even more hurt. More often than not, people are not sure what to say, do, or how to act as they comfort a friend. Do not take their reactions wrong, just play it down and let it go!

Secondly, when you have lost someone you love, it is important to remember that God is in complete control. His timing is perfect, and He does not make mistakes. When my mother died at age 54 after suffering miserably for four years, I had to learn to accept the fact that Mom's perfect healing came in the form of her death. Although it *feels* like things may be spinning out of control at times, the *truth* prevails that God continues to be "large and in charge."

We do not know His plan or purpose as fully as we will someday. Yet for now, our faith in the Bible as the true word of God must carry us through! So the truth is, in Christ, we all have victory over the grave and actually pass from life into life, not life into death! Life with Him, away from the presence and power of sin, is our ultimate reward as Christians—eternity with Christ in heaven!

Finally, I tell the players of something that I am constantly reminding myself to think about. When the death of a loved
one leaves you wondering how you will ever get over it, do not
try to get over it! It is not part of your make up as God's child
to "get over" losing a parent, child, friend, or even a celebrity
you have become attached to on the radio or in the movies.
What I try to think about is this—"You will never 'get over' it,
but you will adjust to it, learn to live with it, and move forward!"

Again, our faith requires us to "press on" when we have
suffered a loss. But God would have us trust, adjust, and stay
true to the joy we have been given in Jesus Christ!

39

Caring in Crisis

There have been many times in my nine seasons with the Denver Nuggets that I have seen grown men cry together. When an injury knocks a player out of action is probably the most common time they cry. To see the dreams of a player left in pieces instantly with a broken bone or torn muscle is sad for the entire team. I have also seen that when any form of crisis occurs on a team many very special things can happen. The love and care that teammates, coaches, and fans give each other is just one example. It is almost as if the tragedy brings out the best in people and causes them to react to each other in more loving and caring ways. I have seen it over and over, and I am sure you have too.

Gari and I have had our share of crisis in our 30 years of marriage. Our love for each other and the faithfulness of Christ in our lives has helped us to overcome painful and difficult situations. We have also experienced great joy, even in the midst of crisis, by the care that we have received from family members and friends.

I love to share with the players at chapel my personal experiences with how caring in crisis can be a wonderful way to reach out to others with the love of Christ. I applaud our players whenever I see them pick up the spirits of a fellow teammate going through a tough time. Strong bonds of love can be established in the midst of a crisis, and as Christians we are called to look for opportunities to serve one another in love!

Margaret, my mother, battled cancer for four long years. In the first few years, there were literally hundreds of people who would stop by to encourage her or bring over food to help. In her last year, she lost about sixty pounds and looked weak and frail. She was bedridden and spoke only in very low, soft tones. You have probably seen someone close to you suffering in this way, so you know how sad it can be to see someone slowly slipping away. Eventually, the only people that kept in touch and continued to come over to see her were the devoted Christians. Why? Because death did not intimidate them! The severity of the crisis caused them to call more, not run away out of fear.

In 1992, my family and I went through a very dark and difficult period brought on by legal issues that came about because of my involvement in some real estate loan transactions. Looking back now, I am glad it all happened because of the way it helped me personally to grow as a Christian. This time of crisis also helped me to grow closer to people I love. One of those people was my daughter Ashley. She cared for and supported me deeply during that time. It is impossible to describe how helpful and loving she was to me. Ashley and I would not be the friends we are today if it were not for that crisis period and the caring love she gave to me. The same is true for my sister, Lana, and her husband Charlie Roskamp. They called, wrote, and let us all know how much they loved us, and their concern lifted us above our circumstances. They are very strong Christians and their faith carried my family and me on days when our emotional tanks were empty. They were there for us and our love for them and their daughters, Natalie and Meredith, was deepened during the crisis and will last forever.

The Bible teaches us that, *"Two are better than one, because they have a good return for their work: If one falls down his friend can help him up. But pity the man who falls and has no one to help him up!"* (Ecclesiastes 4:9-10). Eventually, everyone gets the heart breaking phone call or something terrible happens and they must embrace the awful feelings that crisis brings. Our foundation blocks are checked when crisis hits, and the help we receive from a loving friend at that moment can carry us a long way!

What an honor it is to be the person who lends a helping hand. Why? As Christians, we have answers for those in crisis that can give them an ounce of comfort and a pound of hope! We know what to do and say because of what Jesus has done for us personally. His love is what they need to hear and see to help them make any sense of their crisis.

We do need to be careful though, not to rescue someone out of a difficult situation because Christ may be working deeply in their life in the midst of their suffering. It is usually during those "down" times when people learn the greatest lessons in life because it is then when they are most vulnerable and open to the loving power of Christ.

What an honor it is to represent Christ with people who are hurting! I encourage you to take notice and then to respond when you get the news that a family member or friend is in crisis. You may be "the only Bible they read for a while," and your life and love could have an eternal impact on them. Christ wants to comfort the lonely, confused, scared, and hurting. You and I can be His messengers if in humility and love we reach out to them in His matchless name!

40

The Sermon on the Amount

One night I entered the locker room at about 5:45 p.m. and two of our players were already in the training room getting their ankles taped. I looked over the left shoulder of one of our stars as he was reviewing the stub portion of his paycheck. Near the bottom of the form it showed the amount that he had been paid to that point in the season, approximately $1.2 million. Jokingly, I said softly in his ear, "You are being cheated aren't you—they are not paying you enough." He could tell I was kidding him, and he looked at me kind of funny. I said, "God is good, isn't he," to which my friend replied, "God is very good, and I thank Him."

Most NBA players make millions of dollars per season. Some people are critical of the players for these large salaries. I have never personally felt that way. The fact is, there are only about three or four hundred basketball players in the world talented enough to compete in the NBA. In addition, the players do not establish the market value for their talent. Rather, it is the owners who pay their salaries and the fans who purchase the tickets. So, what are the players supposed to say, "Oh, no, that's way too much, I'll play for much less!" I don't think so!

Each season, I take the opportunity at a chapel to share with the players what the Bible says about how they should handle and manage their money. Most seasons, one or more of the players will privately ask me if I would help them manage their money. In terms of what to do with their money, I always tell them the same thing: tithe cheerfully, give beyond your tithe, pay your taxes, and put what is left in the bank. It is not my role to advise them on investments even if I could. I am their chaplain. But the same advice I give them from the Bible applies to all of us who are doing our best to be good stewards of what God has given us.

First of all, it is okay that we spend a lot of time thinking about money. We should think about how to make it, invest it, save it, give it away, spend it on ourselves, and others. It can occupy a lot of our time. The Bible spends much time on money and materialism. It says in 1 Timothy 6:10, *"The love of money is the root of all evil."* Not money itself, but the *love* of it. This is a foundational truth that must be understood if we are ever going to handle properly what God has given us. It gives us perspective.

God knows we need money to function even if our "minds and hearts are set on things above" (Colossians 3:1). In addition, He is the provider who gives us the minds, health, energy, and ideas to make money. But God is not the one who gets money out of balance. That responsibility is ours, and ours alone. You do not have to be a multimillion dollar athlete to get this critical part of your life out of balance. Anyone can, and all of us seem to do it at some point in our lives.

I have friends in ministry, making a good living but not wealthy, who are actually some of the most materialistic people I know. They love their money and the things they can buy with it. They seem to be unbalanced and unbiblical in the way they look at money management.

The amount you have or make is not the issue; it is your attitude that is the real issue. I have other friends that make a lot more money in the business world than the ball players in my chapel services will ever make, and they are the most balanced Christian managers of God's money you could imagine. In fact, their blessings seem to increase because of their obedience in response to God's plan of economy. I say hooray for them and for God!

Once you trust the fact that God is the provider and that He has entrusted His resources to you for living (needs) and pleasure (wants) you have His foundation for money management. The following are some scriptures that may help you understand God's plan of economy.

DEUTERONOMY 14:22

"Be sure to set aside a tenth of all that your fields produce each year." The launching pad—a minimum!

EXODUS 23:19

"Bring the best of the firstfruits of your soil to the house of the Lord your God." First, not leftovers!

DEUTERONOMY 16:16-17

"No man should appear before the Lord empty handed; each of you must bring a gift in proportion to the way the Lord your God has blessed you." Everyone lives in obedience, not just rich folks!

PROVERBS 11:24-25

"One man gives freely, yet gains even more; another withholds unduly, but comes to poverty. A generous man will prosper; he who refreshes others will himself be refreshed." Give because it is right, but be prepared to receive more!

ECCLESIASTES 11:1-2

"Give generously, for your gifts will return to you later. Divide your gifts among many, for in the days ahead you yourself may need much help." Cheerful giving!

MATTHEW 10:8

"Remember this: Whoever sows sparingly will also reap sparingly, and whoever sows generously will also reap generously. Each man should give what he has decided in his heart to give, not reluctantly or under compulsion, for God loves a cheerful giver."

MARK 12:41-44

"Jesus sat down opposite the place where the offerings were put and watched the crowd putting their money into the temple treasury. Many rich people threw in large amounts. But a poor widow came and put in two very small copper coins, worth only a fraction of a penny. Calling His disciples to him, Jesus said, 'I tell you the truth, this poor widow has put more into the treasury than all the others. They all gave out of their wealth; but she, out of her poverty, put in everything—all she had to live on.'"

Wow! Real power!

There are some things in the Bible that are not clear about how we should conduct ourselves as Christians, but in terms of money, the Bible is very specific and clear.

Acknowledge God's ownership of all that you possess!

> Psalm 24:1
> *"The earth is the Lord's and everything in it, the world, and all who live in it."*
> Haggai 2:8
> *"'The silver is Mine and the gold is Mine,' declares the Lord Almighty."*

Give off the top of the Lord's work!

> Proverbs 3:9-10
> *"Honor the Lord with your wealth, with the firstfruits of all your crops; then your barns will be filled to overflowing, and your vats will brim over with new wine."*

Give beyond that, as a cheerful giver!
Provide for the well being of your family!

> 1 Timothy 5:8
>
> *"If anyone does not provide for his relatives, and especially for his immediate family, he has denied the faith and is worse than an unbeliever."*

I do not tell our players to clear out their bank accounts and give it all away. But it is clear what God expects from each of us as we study His word.

He wants us to give responsibly, so find areas where your help is truly needed. Find organizations that are lifting up the name and causes of Christ and not merely themselves. Study the leadership and the effectiveness of those organizations and then make your decisions to give wisely!

Be astute for this is God's money you are managing. Do not be reckless but be aggressive and give sacrificially, not out of surplus! God often blesses us in the spirit with incredible generosity. It is one of life's great blessings to give to others! It is a blessing to everyone involved.

This little poem says it all and is one of my favorites!

Break for the needy
Sweet charities bread
For "Living is giving"
The angel said
What? Giving, again
I asked in dismay
Must I keep giving
And giving away

Oh, no, said the angel
Piercing me through
Just give till the Father
Stops giving to you!

Author Unknown

41

Sermons We See

One of our star players also happened to be one of the strongest and most consistent Christians in the league. It was very sad for all of us who loved him to see him facing a very difficult knee surgery, that could possibly end his career prematurely. A few nights before the surgery, his wife threw a big "pre-surgery party" for him, his teammates, and a few friends. We had a great time that night just laughing together, playing games, and sharing stories about all kinds of subjects. It was a joy for me to observe my friend, as he interacted with the people he loved the most and with the people who worked at the place where the party was being held. He was incredible! He took the time to make every person feel that they were the most important person in the room. He had just the right hug or a high five for everyone. He had an understanding of how to treat people that caused me to sit back, observe, and celebrate my friend as one of the best examples I have ever seen of a Christian in action.

After the surgery, I visited him in the hospital. It was the second day in a row for me to observe my friend in action. He continued to treat the nurses and doctors in a very kind, special way even though he was experiencing great pain and discomfort. It was incredible to observe him, and I will never forget it!

I was soon able to report to the other guys how their teammate was doing. I also took advantage of the opportunity to brag on my friend's conduct. In fact, I opened chapel by sharing this thought provoking poem by Edgar A. Guest.

I'd rather see a sermon than hear one any day,
I'd rather one should walk with me than merely show the way.
The eye's a better pupil and more willing than the ear;
Fine counsel is confusing, but example's always clear;
And the best of all the preachers are the men who live their creeds,
For to see the good in action is what everybody needs.

I can soon learn how to do it if you'll let me see it done,
I can watch your hand in action, but your tongue too fast may run;
And the lectures you deliver may be very wise and true;
But I'd rather get my lesson by observing what you do;
For I may misunderstand you and the high advice you give,
But there's no misunderstanding how you act and how you live.

I've been taught that 7% of what we actually communicate comes from the words we say. The other 93% of our communication comes from our tone of voice and our body language. As an example, in a gruff voice, with a scowl on your face and your arms folded you can look at a friend and say, "I told you, I love you!" With that kind of body language and tone of voice, I doubt your friend believes you truly love him!

In an effort to *"please Him always in everything we do,"* 2 Corinthians 5:9, it is imperative that our "walk" with Christ be consistent with our "talk." Therefore, it is sometimes better not to do too much "talking" before we have actually "walked" as a Christian long enough to know that our behavior, speech and conduct is consistent with a life that is pleasing to Christ.

During a baseball game in college, I struck out on a called third strike that I thought was way over my head. Without hesitation, I turned to the umpire and told him where he could put his 3rd strike, along with a few other not so loving wise cracks. Well, he was forced to throw me out of the game. I spent the rest of the afternoon on the bench wondering how I would explain this to my friend and spiritual mentor, Coach Dan Stavely. He was picking me up at 8:00 a.m. the next morning to speak at Southern Hills Baptist church about my walk with Christ, a test of which I had flunked miserably during that college game. I guess I still needed to mature in this area.

We've all blown it and lived to regret it! The players and I established a goal that night of memorizing "Sermons We See" as a helpful tool to be used for the rest of our lives as a constant reminder not to be inconsistent in our walk with Christ. Our "walk" needs to match up with our "talk" because we truly are a sermon to everyone we meet.

"So our aim is to please him always in everything we do, whether we are here in this body or away from this body and with him in heaven."

2 Corinthians 5:9

42

Heads Up!

I used to love to watch Magic Johnson when he played for the L.A. Lakers and especially when he would come to town to take on the Nuggets. He was my son's favorite player, and obviously one of the greatest players to ever play the game. What I noticed about Magic's play was how he played the game with his head up. He seemed to be aware of every other player on the court at any given time. He was one of the greatest assist men in history because he kept his head up and knew when and where the next pass should go. As great as he was individually, his primary contribution to the Lakers was how he made everyone around him better than they normally would have been.

It occurred to me one night while observing Magic, that the world would be a better place if we all lived daily with our heads up! Not literally, but actually thinking of others and focusing on them and not just ourselves. We all could make an effort to lift our eyes, hearts, and minds! In the *Living Bible*, Philippians 2:2-4 says, *"Then make me truly happy by loving each other and agreeing wholeheartedly with each other, waking together with one heart and mind and purpose. Don't be selfish; don't live to make a good impression on others. Be humble, thinking of others as better than yourself. Don't just think of your own affairs, but be interested in others, too, and in what they are doing."* There it is! A description of how we would think and conduct ourselves if we lived with our "heads up." We would be much more tuned in to people and their needs. We would be like Christ in developing what my friend, Bobb Biehl, calls "You Focus." "You Focus" describes a mind that is more interested in others than yourself. It becomes a way of thinking, acting, and living.

One season the Nuggets team had been bickering with each other for weeks. We were playing Dallas on a Saturday night, and I decided that afternoon to do the most peculiar thing I had ever done in all my years as a chaplain. To make the point that we needed to start playing and living our lives as Christians with our "heads up," I decided to bring my guitar to chapel and sing to the guys. I was apprehensive about this so I called my son, Andy, and asked him what he thought about the idea. He said, "It sounds a little strange, Dad. They'll probably laugh you out of the place!" My wife agreed, yet I had a feeling that the drastic state of affairs with the team chemistry required a drastic move on my part—ridiculous or not!

If you could find the players who attended chapel that Saturday night, I am sure they would remember what happened. They might not remember the point of my message, but they would remember the guitar and singing. As they filtered into chapel, a couple of them picked up my guitar and broke into a brief jam session. It was fun to see them laughing and enjoying each other in contrast to their normal bickering and pre-game silence. After things settled down, I turned out the lights and lit a candle in the center of the room. Even though I am not a good singer or guitar player, I began to sing and play the popular song by the Judds, "Love Can Build a Bridge." The chorus repeats over and over that "Love can build a bridge, between your heart and mine, love can build a bridge, don't you think it's time, don't you think it's time." I could tell by the silence and respect they showed me that they were getting the message. They overlooked my lousy singing and focused on the message. It was there that they began to rid themselves of their inverted eyeballs and started focusing on their teammates. I suggested to them that men say "I love you" to each other with "high-fives" and pats on the back. I then gave them a piece of paper and asked them to write down the name of their least favorite teammate.

That night, I took each piece of paper and carefully destroyed them one by one. The players knew their task was to reach out to the person whose name they had written down.

Maybe you need to start there too. Make a list and begin tomorrow with a call or a letter of love, make an effort to reach out to those whom you need to forgive or love in a new way. If you do not know what to say, just try your best to say something that is loving and kind.

The men in chapel that night are wonderful people, but we all can fall into the trap of self-centeredness, and it is usually the first step towards all kinds of sin. God wants us to lead the charge by being love brokers to a world in great need! He teaches us how to love others unconditionally. To follow his example we must raise our heads, eyes, hearts and minds to see the need around us in the faces of our families, friends, and fellowman!

People are waiting for Christians to become bridge builders between their hearts, our hearts, and the heart of God!

43

Fatherhood

My dad's name was Dale Mitchell, and he played ten years in the major leagues with the Cleveland Indians and the Brooklyn Dodgers. He was a tremendous player with a lifetime batting average of .312. He was sold to the Dodgers in the summer of 1956 and on October 8th in the fifth game of the World Series, Yankee pitcher Don Larson struck my dad out to end the only perfect game in World Series history. After a lifetime of achievement and success, he is mostly remembered by baseball fans as "the last batter in Don Larson's perfect game."

When I was growing up, everyone in Oklahoma seemed to know our family because of my dad's fame as a baseball player. He was born and raised in a tiny shack in western Oklahoma, and the spotlight was quite a change for him. He handled it well however, and everyone loved him, especially me. Because his own father had died when Dad was just a kid himself, he had little training on how to be a father. However, to me, he was always a great Daddy and Dad!

Dad always called me "running mate." Ballplayers usually pair up with a buddy to run their sprints in the outfield grass for conditioning purposes. The teammate you choose to run with is called your "running mate." It always made me feel great when Dad called me by that nickname. I remember, too, that Paul Peterson had a hit song in the 50's called "My Dad." The words to the song said, "when I was small I felt ten feet tall when I walked by his side—when everyone would say that's his son—my heart would burst with pride!" That is how my Dad made me feel growing up, and until the day he died of a heart attack in 1987, he was my hero, and he was special.

Most of the players in the NBA are married with small children. I feel it is important each year to spend one chapel service discussing the importance of fatherhood. I begin chapel by telling our players the story of our good friend, Helen Dye. When Ashley was five and Andy was three, she pointed out to me that I was not doing a good job at all in terms of raising our children. She said I was so focused on my business that I had no real knowledge or understanding of my kids' lives. Her council led Gari and me to reprioritize our lives with a new focus on Christ, our marriage, and our children. Fortunately, Ashley and Andy were young enough that I did not miss much of their childhood. Gari had actually been in the right mindset from the beginning. She seemed to know almost everything our kids needed from a mom. In fact, she said to me on more than one occasion, "Bo, you go do all you need to do, but I am staying home and raising our kids!" So, I was the problem! I was the one miserably failing prior to Helen's helpful advice. Fortunately, I can look back now with joy instead of regret, because my children say to me that I became a good dad, and I thank God, Gari, Helen, and the kids that I did not completely blow it!

I go on to teach the players a lesson that comes from a concept a friend named Bob Beltz and I developed in the early '80's. We had seen an interview Barbara Walters conducted with the actor Burt Reynolds. She asked him, "How would you like to be remembered?" His response was an eye opener for Bob and me. He said, "I would like to be remembered as a great daddy!" (Not great "Dad," but great "Daddy.")

Bob and I discussed this interview and were struck with the notion that the period when we are called "Daddy" is different from the period when we are called "Dad." The "Daddy" period of time seems to go from birth until a child is eight, nine, or ten, and then a man becomes "Dad."

In fact, we went on to understand that almost every single relationship with problems can be reconciled and made whole, except this one, because this relationship happens in a specific period of time, and we cannot go back when the time has past. We are Mom and Dad for a lifetime, but "Mommy" and "Daddy" for just a few short years.

So, the problem is this. At the same period in life that we are building our marriages and our careers, too often our young children are neglected. In the case of the NBA players, the travel demands alone can put a strain on their ability to be great "Daddies" if they are not paying close attention!

The mistake of neglecting our children is usually not intentional, but it happens. As in my case, men need to be encouraged to concentrate on this incredibly important role—the role of "Daddy." They also need role models showing them how to balance all of their career demands with the priority always on the family.

I have heard it said that, "No success at the office can compensate for failure at home." I agree with this statement and it is a lesson that we can learn from before the problem negatively effects our kids. They truly are the most precious and important gifts God gives us on earth, and placing a priority on fatherhood is the first step for men to take in an effort to successfully do our part in being the daddies and dads our kids deserve and need us to be.

Post Season

44

Communication

I read a quote years ago from the author John Powell that said, "Communication is the life-blood of love." This quote stuck with me, and I believe it to be true. I also believe our individual communication skills to be something that we can all work on and improve throughout our lives. Therefore, the importance of communication has become a topic in chapel each year, as I continue to attempt to impart interesting, important, life changing skills to the Denver Nuggets players.

To begin with, since I have such a brief time in a chapel service, I only touch on two areas of communication. The first and most important one is prayer, which is our communication with God. The second area I touch on is communication with each other.

Prayer. It is how we talk with God, and it is how we are able to listen to Him. Are you not amazed? Are you not overwhelmed with the idea that you can have dialog with the Creator and Author of life? It is almost too much to comprehend. Yet, millions of people live their lives without ever acting on the availability of prayer for communication with God.

Most of the guys I meet in chapel are not used to much praying. Some do pray with their children before bed. Others may utter a quick prayer on the court just before the game starts or before a key free throw. But they all seem to listen as I give a few thoughts as to what God says in the Bible our prayer life should look like, because for most of us, how much, when and how we pray does not measure up to what God would have us do.

First, I teach the players that God must always be approached reverently and respectfully. Then I explain the "A.C.T.S." method of prayer. This method is helpful for people who have never prayed, or for those of us who sometimes just do not know where to start. This method of prayer has helped many deepen their prayer life and therefore deepen their walk with Christ.

"A" stands for *adoration*. This is the spirit we should have when we pray. When we say phrases like, "I adore you, I love you, I lift up your name," we posture ourselves before God in an attitude of admiration and respect. That is why we pray on our knees; it positions us in humility before God. What position you are in when you pray is not critical, but when you pray on your knees it is a physical reminder of who you are and who God is!

"C" stands for *confession*. This is where prayer begins to clean us and make us fresh. To confess in prayer is to say to God, "I'm sorry and my intent is to never do it again." He responds to those cries by erasing our sins! It is like He put a big fire hose down our throats and flushes us out from head to toe! We receive a clean slate, a white washed new beginning. First John 1:9 says, *"If we confess our sins, he is faithful and just and will forgive us our sins and purify us from all unrighteousness."*

Too often, people get stuck on this aspect of prayer. "Oh, no, not me. I've been too awful in my life to ask for God's forgiveness." Well, the humility involved with coming to God and asking for forgiveness is exactly what he says for us to do in his own examples of prayer. *"Forgive us our trespasses as we forgive those who trespass against us."* Matthew 6:12. It is the very reason He went to the cross, so do not leave Him hanging there! Confession and the forgiveness that follows is like when you press the "clear" button on a calculator. All of the incorrect information you wanted to erase is gone, lost forever. That is what happens to sin when God forgives us!

"T" stands for *thanksgiving* and is easily understood. We have so many things to be thankful for, and God loves to hear us remember them in prayer. He is the creator of everything good in this world. Let us give thanks to Him!

"S" stands for *supplication,* which is defined by how we pray for others and ask Him to assist, protect and draw them close to Himself. Supplication is also fairly easy to grasp, because it is the concept of getting in line to petition Christ on behalf of other people. It is meaningful for people to know you have prayed for them, to know you care.

Prayer is the life-blood we need to communicate with God and grow closer. Where you pray does not really matter—in your car, at your desk, walking with your child or wife—the point is, come to God through prayer, and talk to Him! Practice is also critical! The more you pray the better you will be. Start where you are, even if that is just saying, "Father, I don't get it, but help me to understand how this works."

Along with prayer, communication with each other is also critical if we are to live fulfilled lives as Christians. We would not get very close to each other if we did not communicate. I enjoy making the phone calls or writing the notes that may lift someone's spirits. I consider it a privilege not a burden. However, communication with others requires commitment of time, energy, and thought. But in the long run, we are the ones blessed by becoming great communicators.

One rule I try to live by in communication is this: "If it's positive write it down and if it's negative, play it down and pray it up!" This helps me to remember to thank people or celebrate them when I see or hear something good about them. I especially like to write notes for the purpose of clarity. It is like a welcome gift to someone when you take the time to write or say, "I thank you or I heard about this great thing you did." The other side is also true. If it is negative, just play it down and pray it up! Do not dwell on it. Gari, my wife, says negative words you say can float around for a long time, causing problems wherever they land, and you cannot retrieve them. They are like feathers tossed into the wind.

Therefore, prayer is the key, as we learn from God all He would have us to know, and communication with each other is critical. Even though communication can be difficult at times and takes effort, we should all have the common goal of becoming great communicators!

I encourage you to make an effort to become a great communicator! Come to God in prayer. Love people by writing to them and telling them the great things they do and how wonderful they are!

Off Season

45

Game Over

When it is obvious to the players involved in the action that something has just occurred to seal the outcome of the game, often times someone says, "Game over!" It has come to mean, "That's it, it's final, that's all there is to it!" It is also used in the NBA in conversation when someone hits a three point shot to put the score out of reach and seal the victory.

At the conclusion of each season, I leave the players with something they can build on during the off season. I know in many cases it is going to be five or six months until I will see them again, so I make the last chapel a challenging and memorable one. I ask them to think about their lives in terms of when they die. I ask them to project into the future a time when they know they will hear the words, "Game over," and their time on earth is almost finished. Then I ask them to think about what they should focus on <u>now</u> in order not to be disappointed <u>later</u> with how they lived their lives.

In this final chapel, the first thing I share with them is the last letter I received from my mother, Margaret Mitchell, just a few days before she died in September, 1976. She was a very dedicated Christian, and my memories of her are wonderful. She was one of the most loving and giving people I have ever met but could also be plenty tough. The last four years of her life, she battled cancer. She suffered horribly, and her perfect healing came in the form of death at age 54. Dale Sr., my dad,

Lana, my sister, Dale Jr., my brother, and I were with her as much as possible for the two years leading up to her death. On the Sunday night she wrote the following letter, she was a woman who thought that she might "pass out this time and not pull back out of it." In other words, as you read this letter, understand that my mom thought she might die at any moment.

Sunday, 1:00 a.m.

Dear Dale and Kids,

I'm sitting on the floor on a pad and pillow—Dr. Hidy is out of town but someone will stand in for him if I wind up back in the hospital.

I have seen all of you this week except Gari. I'm writing because I feel pretty weak—anything could happen. I could pass out this time and not pull back out of it.

Dale, this accounts for my 100-pulse rate. I felt it come down the same way as two weeks ago.

I talked to Mom tonight—earlier.

There's money in my billfold.

You know where things are and what to do—don't anyone fall apart—they will keep me comfortable and that means a lot to me.

There is a letter in the old Bible. Bury this one with me.

Try to be a strong family. *Know how I feel about so many things being worse than death.*

No one could love you all more than I do—on this earth that is.

We will just pray that I get through this night here at home. Glad Bo is here if I get hauled to hospital. You'd have to call Waldo or Woodie early to get Mom here.

Lana—don't forget   P.S.—Jean gets sack
   Grandma's gown   of needlepoint.
   and robe set.

Love,
Mom

There are so many wonderful things that this letter reveals. Her care for others and the loving way she is still instructing and directing us all in the smallest details. Her love for her kids and her mention of prayer as to how she might get through the night. Even the fact that she does not want to wake us up to help her, but chooses to battle alone, not to disturb anyone. She was always giving in her concern for others over her own well-being. But the one line that speaks volumes to me is when she says "Know how I feel about so many things being worse than death." She is almost hearing the words, "Game over" and yet has no fear. Why? She lived her life in a growing relationship with Christ! She knew *exactly* where she was going, and even though she would miss us, she was encouraging us to understand that we pass from life to life, not life to death.

The Bible teaches in 2 Corinthians 5:8 that to be *"absent from the body is to be present with the Lord."* My mom knew that, felt it, could sense it, and it was about to happen for her while she was writing this last letter to her family. Wow! What a legacy she left! Because her name is written in the Book of Life and because she belonged to Jesus, she *knew* that her tombstone would not be filled with a bunch of empty, meaningless words. In fact, one word could have covered it, "Vacant." Obviously, that's not what it says, but she knew that would have been accurate! She was going to heaven!

If we freely believe the claims and live with the intent daily of serving Him, we should all have this same attitude as we near death. We should have no regrets about how we have lived. More importantly, we should live *now* with an eye towards that day when we will meet Jesus and this "game" as we know it, will be over. We are all going to die, and when we die, death does not determine which direction we go. It merely sets into place for all time the direction we have already chosen!

I encourage you, just as I encourage our players each year, not to waste another moment out of balance on the things of this world. Discipline your minds and hearts to do and say the things that are pleasing to Him, and by doing so you can live the most successful and fulfilling life available this side of heaven!